Marching on Tanga

MARCHING
ON TANGA

BY THE SAME AUTHOR

PROSE

    THE YOUNG PHYSICIAN
    THE CRESCENT MOON
    THE IRON AGE
    THE DARK TOWER
    DEEP SEA
    UNDERGROWTH (With E. BRETT YOUNG)
    ROBERT BRIDGES: A CRITICAL STUDY

POETRY

    FIVE DEGREES SOUTH

IN PREPARATION

POEMS: 1916-1918

Extra Cr. 8vo.   5/- *net*

W. COLLINS · SONS & CO. LTD.

MARCHING ON TANGA

WITH GENERAL SMUTS IN EAST AFRICA

By FRANCIS BRETT YOUNG

NEW AND REVISED EDITION ILLUSTRATED
IN COLOUR BY JOHN E. SUTCLIFFE AND
WITH MANY PHOTOGRAPHS AND MAP

LONDON   48 PALL MALL   MCMXIX
WILLIAM COLLINS SONS & CO. LTD.
GLASGOW   MELBOURNE   AUCKLAND

TO MY FRIEND
STEPHEN REYNOLDS

My dear *Reynolds,—They jolted my poor body
up the Tanga Line in one of their damned cattle-
trucks, and shot me out into a Stationary Hospital
at M'buyuni, where the big baobab stood. I crawled
into a bed in which there were real sheets; and when
I woke next morning in a mild and very peaceful
light, I found that they had put a book on the table
at my bedside. . . . It was one of your own books,
and not, I think, a very good one; but I read it all
the same (I who had read no book for many months
but a map of England!), and found, to my sudden
joy, that I was meeting a friend. For this book,
whatever else it contained, held a great deal of your-
self; so that, reading it, I could imagine that we
were talking together, as we three have talked so
many times, above my blue bay, in the soft western
weather. It was so good and so homely that I felt
I must thank you: and so I, too, am going to send
you this twice-torpedoed once-rewritten book, in the
hope that it may some day serve as happy a purpose
as your own*

Yours *as ever,*

FRANCIS BRETT YOUNG.

COLOURED ILLUSTRATIONS

BLACK AND WHITE ILLUSTRATIONS

THE GIFT

Marching on Tanga, marching the parched plain
Of wavering spear-grass past Pangani river,
England came to me—me who had always ta'en
But never given before—England, the giver,
In a vision of three poplar trees that shiver
On still evenings of summer, after rain,
By Slapton Ley, where reed-beds start and quiver
When scarce a ripple moves the upland grain.
Then I thanked God that now I had suffered pain
And, as the parched plain, thirst, and lain awake
Shivering all night through till cold daybreak
In that I count these sufferings my gain
And her acknowledgment.   Nay, more, would fain
Suffer as many more for her sweet sake.

Under Old Lassiu.
June 1916.

CHAPTER I

WHEN the troop train ran into the siding at Taveta the dawn was breaking. All through the night we had been moving by fits and starts over the new military line from Voi, moving through a dark and desolate land which, eighteen months before, had been penetrated by very few men indeed. In that night journey we could see little of the country. Not that we slept—our progress was too freakish, and the Indian railway trucks in which we were packed were too crowded for that—but because the night seemed to lie upon it with a peculiar heaviness All the time one was conscious, without seeing them, of the imminence of vast mountain masses, even though our line carried us for the most part over a fairly open plain. One was conscious, I say, of all these heavy mountains to the north: first the Burra Hills, and later the bulk of Kilimanjaro itself; and when, at a little after five o'clock, the sky began to lighten, we could see that the plain through which we moved was scattered with smaller hills of symmetrical, volcanic shape, to the very summits of which the thick bush climbed.

In the shape of these hillocks there was nothing unusual, for isolated fragments of this kind are scattered over a great part of Africa; but to the men with whom I was travelling, and to whose fortunes for many months to come my own must be linked, these hills bore a very different significance. The smooth green knoll past which we now crept was Salaita, the scene of a most bitter reverse and of a bloodless victory. The wooded crest which marked our southern horizon, two gentle summits with a dip between, was the ridge of Latema, in the Kitowo Hills, blocking that gate between Kilimanjaro and the Pare Mountains which had been forced six weeks before upon the eve of the rains. The nek of Latema-Reata meant a great deal to my companions the Rhodesians. In that fight, when things were going badly, an officer and seventeen men of the regiment had held the narrow passage for hours; and that, so we were told, had been the turning-point in the action which unlocked the gate and made our new invasion possible.

Nearly all the men in the regiment had fought at Salaita and Latema, and, what is more than that, had undergone the weary months of waiting before, when, after the failure before Tanga, everything was touch-and-go in East Africa. When almost daily the Uganda line had been raided by small parties of German askaris, when Mombasa and Nairobi had been equally threatened by an enemy superior in numbers, they had clung to and held that immense defensive line, wanting provisions, wanting water, wanting the very next necessity of life in those parts, quinine. All these privations the Second Rhodesia Regiment had suffered. The unit which left Salisbury over eight hundred strong, moved down after their six months' rest in the highlands with a strength of just under six hundred rifles. At the time when I left them, and at which this narrative will close, they could not put into the firing line more than fifty men; their machine-guns had been returned to Ordnance for want of gunners, and pestilence had swept away the lives of all their transport animals. But they had fulfilled their destiny, which was to be the tempered spear-head of the First Brigade: the weapon which in three months was driven to the heart of the German province.

The move which had cast us so suddenly into Taveta, ahead of the other units of the First Division, was characteristic of the secrecy and swiftness with which Jan Smuts works. Indeed, we were not quite

assured that the greater rains were spent and that
an advance on a large scale would be possible. We
had expected to lie for a week or two at M'buyuni,
where the forces of invasion were concentrating,
until the weather had hardened and the ways were
sure, and on that morning at Taveta the Pare Hills,
a fine fantastic tangle of mountain to the southward, from which blue vapours lazily uncurled,
wore a very watery look, while of Kilimanjaro itself
nothing could be seen, for even the nearer foothills
were half veiled in mist. Yet, though the weather
were doubtful there was no manner of doubt in the
minds of those who were returning to our adventure.
This campaign was to be so different . . . so very
different. To begin with, we should no longer
starve : for great accumulations of animal and
mechanical transport were being massed behind us ;
nor need we lack for men since the South African
contingent—a force as large as our own—was in
the field ; cavalry too would now be at hand to
complete the work of the infantry battalions. Brits,
we were told, was arriving or had even arrived in
Mombasa with his mounted men. It is strange in
these later days to remember how much we staked
on Brits and the Second Mounted Brigade. . . .
But I think that the thing which most sustained

our confidence and made us embark with such high hopes upon the second phase of the East African operations was our absolute confidence in the leadership of Smuts. That he was a fine strategist, the move on Moshi, in spite of the failure of the northern enveloping column, had shown us. Of his personal courage we had been assured by the incidents of the Lumi fight ; but there was yet another factor— in this case one might almost have called it a personal attribute—in his success which demanded our confidence, and that was the luck which has followed him throughout his career. Every one believed in his fortune no less than in his attainments; and it was partly this belief that sent us so happily on our way, for Fortune is the deity of all others whose shrines are never desolate in these precarious days.

In Taveta itself, at the time when we arrived, there was little enough to be seen. It has never had anything to show for its importance on the map but a little mission-station on the crown of a low hill, lying in the marches above the Lumi, as the knoll of Brent lies in the turf-moors at the foot of Mendip. There, indeed, there were trenches and the bleached bones of German dead ; but the old station had been found so pestilential that ever

since our second occupation it had been abandoned
in favour of the open and higher ground over which
the military railway with its network of sidings had
sprawled.

In the new Taveta there was no building except
a deserted hospital, on the roof of which the
Germans, during their occupation, had painted the
symbol which they respect so rarely.   Nor was
there any other sign of life in all that place, apart
from the little group of grass *bandas* which an Indian
casualty clearing station had erected, and another
cluster about the mouth of a well of sweet water,
sunk by the engineers a month or so before.   In
the neighbourhood of this well, the cool water of
which we often remembered in after days, stood a
number of huge galvanised tanks, and when the
men who were working at the well's mouth moved
them they made a sound not unlike that of distant
gunfire, so that once or twice we were tricked into
wondering whether our artillery were not in action
somewhere over in the hills and the great advance
begun without us.

A very few hours after our arrival the Rhodesian
stores and mules had been detrained, a small village
of tents had arisen on the open ground within the
mud perimeter wall at the back of the pumping-

. . . the Rhodesian stores and mules had been detrained (*p.* 6)

station; and as the day advanced, the canvas which had been crinkled like the wings of butter-flies newly fledged, grew smooth, and shone in the sun with a blinding whiteness. The mists, too, which had half concealed the Pare Mountains, were drunk up by the sun, and the lovely out-lines of these hills stood revealed, very blue and beautiful in the distance. But we had other things to think of than their beauty. Somewhere in that tangle of hills great forces of the enemy lay. Only a little the other side of the Lumi, a swift river whose bridges were held by our men, an enemy blockhouse on the spurs of the foothills kept watch over Taveta. Even now they must be watching our white canvas stretched out in the sun, and further to the south the great city of tents at M'buyuni, that standing menace which we had passed in the night. Somehow we had to drive the enemy from those hills, even if our columns were pushed into their utmost recesses; and, as I have said, they were fine rugged mountains, and hard enough to climb without the discouragement of maxim fire.

But more than the distant masses of the Pare, more even than Lake Chala, that secret jewel, the dense forest that lies about the lower waters of the

B

Lumi called me. From our camp at Taveta we
could see the edge of it, low, and blue-black against
the scorched grass of the plain. A road, a rusty
earthen road, ran towards it from the neighbourhood of the empty hospital, winding through the
coarse grass of the swamp, where many herds of
goats were grazing, and always gently falling towards the level of the river. Here, in the open
plain, the heat of the sun was very cruel, the way
interminable, and to reach the shade of the forest
edge was a great relief. Between the rough grass
of the swamp and the edge of the forest lay no
gradations of lesser trees nor even of open bush :
so that one passed directly from the glare of the
sun into a sort of green gloom which was very grateful. But the thing which marked the change from
swamp to forest even more clearly than the lessen-
ing of the light was the sudden silence into which
one entered. Out in the swamp, even without
knowing it, one's ears had been accustomed to the
innumerable murmurs of winged life. Here the
silence was as profound as that which slumbers at
the bottom of the sea, in great depths where there
is no life at all. The trunks of the trees stood
as motionless as though they had been carved out
of coral, and the lianas with which they were

hung seemed as little alive as the painted foliage
of a theatre : for in these lower levels of the forest
no breath of air stirred. It was only when I raised
my eyes to the great heights above me that I
realised wherein the forest had its life. In that
remote clerestory a wealth of life moved. There
there were birds—and notably the pied hornbill,
totem of the Wa-Taveta ; there the gaudy floaters
spread their wings ; there all the beauty of the
forest flowered, expanding under the light of the
sun. Down below in the deep silence, I became
conscious of a hidden energy, of the thin sap straining upwards, of everything reaching upwards. . . .

I walked a little way into the forest until I became aware of the sound of running water, and at
length pushed my way to the bank of a swift
stream. This was the Lumi, a brown river rushing
between steep banks. At the point where I struck
it the water swirled into a deep pool, and the sunlight, which here beat vertically upon its surface
through the parting of the trees, showed a bottom
of tawny sand dappled with light which tempted
me to bathe. While I was standing here entranced
with that race of brown water and its noise, another
sound came to my ears, the beating of a distant
drum. Over there, somewhere in the heart of the

forest, an *N'goma* was being held. How far away it might be I could not guess, but it was a thrilling sound that would not let me be until I had traced it to its source. The only thing about its direction that was certain was that it lay somewhere beyond the river.

In three places I tried to make a crossing, and once, indeed, I thought I had succeeded, only to find that the arm which I had crossed was nothing more than a creek or backwater of the main stream. It seemed that the river here made a loop, and that the sound of drumming came from the middle of the peninsula which it enfolded. At last, in the midst of a swiftly flowing rapid, I came to a place where a tree had been felled by fire. Above the bank where it lay the red earth was trampled, and by this I knew that it had been meant for a bridge. I crossed it, though this was no easy matter, and thrusting again into the forest found that the peninsula was nothing more than a great swamp full of marshy air. From among the trunks of the greater trees all undergrowth had been cleared away, and bananas had been planted in thousands. In their struggle to reach the sun these plantations had grown to a great height, and their flat fleshy leaves shut out the little light which filtered through. It was a strange and gloomy place, in which one gasped for air. The soil was all oozy and black and trodden with such a maze of twisting paths that one could not tell where to go.

For a mile or so I steered by the sound of drumming, which never ceased, and I cannot say that it ever seemed to grow nearer. It seemed that one could wander for hours and hours in this forest and never find a village. But at last I saw between the trees a moving procession; a small naked boy driving a herd of nearly a hundred goats. In his hand he carried a little spear. Now, at any rate, I argued, I must be near some village, for the udders of the goats were full, and they were surely being driven home to be milked. The naked boy was not afraid of me. He raised his hand to his brow in salutation. I gave him '*Jambo*,' to which he replied, and I followed it up with the conventional '*Habari gani*?' 'What's the news?' '*M'zuri*' . . . 'Good,' says he. And we left it at that.

I followed the oozy path which he was taking, and then, all of a sudden, became aware that the drumming was very near. And now there was another sound, the shrill scream of a woman in pain. My small herdsman took no heed of these things:

he had more serious work in hand. It was so dark beneath the flat banana leaves that I could scarcely see. I had come to a little clearing in the forest in the centre of which the drummer stood. He was a man of middle age, and beat with his hands upon a goatskin stretched over a tree-trunk hollowed by fire which he held between his knees. The rhythm which he hammered out upon this drum, and which never changed, although the vehemence of his beating was often varied, was what musicians call 'three-eight' time: a succession of galloping triplets, almost continuous, with the faintest possible emphasis on the first note of every three. While he played his drum he sang to a tune as monotonous as his rhythm certain words which did not resemble any sounds in Ki-swahili which I knew. At his side a younger boy crouched, beating out the same rhythm upon an empty German petrol tin, while a second child, standing beside the drum, supplied a sort of syncopated accompaniment to his father's drumming. None of these male performers seemed to take the business very seriously: the man smiled at me, and the boys stared, though their hands were still busy. But with the women, of whom there were a great many more, the dance was a far more serious affair.

Perhaps there were twenty of them of every age from puberty to extreme old age. They were almost naked, and not one of them could have been considered physically attractive in any degree apart from one young girl, decorated as a bride, whose body had a certain yielding grace. It was she, poor thing, whom I had heard screaming in the depths of the wood. When I came near to their circle she was just recovering from the ecstasy into which she had been thrown. She lifted herself from the ground and staggered in a dazed fashion to the line of other women, taking her place next to an ancient creature who was working her withered hips as though the whole thing were an unconscionable bore which it was her duty to countenance. But the wretched girl at her side could not treat the matter so lightly. She had a ridiculously small shaven head, which reminded me of the heads of the Mantis family of insects—so small that only an insect's intelligence could hide within it. It was this head which she began to move in time to the drum music, and with her head her whole body swayed. Then, one by one, the different parts of her body and her limbs took up the rhythm, gently at first, but later with a devastating intensity until, at last, the whole organism was possessed by that overmastering music, and to the movements which marked the bars was added a series of subordinate twitches representing the bar's individual notes, so that the woman's body was nothing but a mass of ghastly quivering muscles. Perhaps it was the stifling air of the place imprisoned by the flat banana leaves, perhaps the slightly sickening odour of black flesh, and above all that devilish rhythm from which there was no escape, but in any case I experienced a feeling very near to physical nausea. And the woman was suffering too. She clutched at her breasts, with hands that were not her own, as though she must try to tear the devil from her ; and then there was wrung from her lips a shrill shuddering cry which was like no human voice. She fell to the ground, and lay there still twitching. But even then the music would not let her be. It seemed as if she could not more utterly surrender herself to its possession, and yet some impulse forced her to crawl towards the drum itself and thrust her tortured head within the hollow trunk beneath it.

Even on a spectator the awful monotony of the rhythm had begun to exercise some hypnotic effect. It seemed as if the business could not go on much longer without something happening beyond one's strict control. There could be no other end to it.

I remembered suddenly certain meadows of my childhood where there was a waterwheel, and a most placid mill-pond, spanned in its narrowest part by a bridge of planking. I remembered how I used to stand at one end of the plank and set it vibrating, gently at first, and then, little by little, more violently, until beneath the cumulative strain it seemed as if the plank must give at last and be broken. The strain of this dominating rhythm was something like that. I wondered how much more of it the girl with the head of an insect could stand. And then, suddenly, the music stopped. For several minutes afterwards the muscles of the possessed continued to twitch, and then, at last, she gave a shuddering sigh and lay still.

The man gave me a courteous greeting. I asked him what kind of *N'goma* this might be. A devil dance, said he. His speech was very difficult for me to understand; but at length I realised that the devil which they were exorcising, the devil which was supposed to escape from the tortured bodies of the women in the cries which they uttered, was the devil of fever. In his village, he told me, there were many sick, and many more had died. And then I saw for the first time how terribly ill and emaciated all that little company looked, and

the awful atmosphere of that village was borne in
on me in the picture of this small community living
miserably in the twilight of their banana swamp,
stubbornly fighting an enemy from whom they
could never escape.   Under the flat banana leaves
it was now growing very dark : the air was laden
with the smell of the dancers' flesh.   I was glad to
leave them and their horror, for in a little while
mosquitoes would take the air, and I was not eager
to try conclusions with their devil.

And that is why I have related this incident at
such length : that in all this campaign our most
deadly enemy was not the human foe who stubbornly retreated before us, but this same devil of
fever who had laid waste that miserable village community in the Lumi swamp.   Already I had been
prepared to meet him ; but this was the first time
that I had looked upon his face, and realised how
terrible was the power he wielded.

CHAPTER II

WHEN I emerged from the stifling atmosphere of
the forest, I found that it was a good deal earlier
than I had imagined under the shadows of the
trees. It was not nearly sunset, and yet the sun
had sunk so low that the land was wrapped in a
mellow light, having reached that hour of the day
which is most grateful in the tropics, when to all
living things that have lain prostrate beneath the
sun's power there comes a sudden and sweet relief.

In this delightful hour I set off again up the
slope towards Taveta, which lay very small and flat
beneath the edge of wooded hills. At first I did not
guess the reason for this change of perspective, for
the place seemed much humbler than when I had
left it—but suddenly I realised that since I had
been away the foothills had become darker, and
more plain ; and as I walked onwards through the
swamp the curtains of mist were very gently lifted,
disclosing blue forest lawns which I had not imagined
to be there. These foothills, it seemed, were greater
far than I had supposed. Out of the mist range
after range materialised, until, through those dis-

solving veils there loomed a shape far mightier than
any which my brain could have conceived : Kilimanjaro, the greatest mountain of all Africa.   Now
that the sun had quite gone from our lowly sight,
the glaciers on the fluted crater of Kibo shone with
an amazing whiteness, while the snows of the sister
peak, Mawenzi, were cold in shade.

The magnitude of these lovely shapes was overwhelming, for they do not rise, as do the other
African peaks, from the base of a mountainous
tableland, but from the edge of a low plain, not
two thousand feet above the sea-level.   Since then
I have seen the great mountain in many guises :
as a dim ghost dominating the lower waters of the
Pangani ; as a filmy cone, imponderable as though
it were carven out of icy vapours, gleaming upon
hot plains a hundred miles away ; as the shadow
which rises from the level skylines of the great game
reserve ; but never did it seem so wonderful as
on that night when it was first revealed to me,
walking from the Lumi forest to Taveta.   There
was indeed something ceremonious in its unveiling,
and the memory of that vast immanence coloured
all the evening of our departure.

For, while I had been away in the forest, Taveta
had greatly changed.   On the open ground next to

. . . a shape far mightier than any which my brain could have conceived (*p.* 18)

our camp a city of tents had arisen. All through the afternoon new units of the First Brigade had been arriving over the road from M'buyuni, and now the place buzzed like a hive. Over that road of red earth there hung a cloud of dust which must have been visible to the German watchers on the Pare. In the open space below the pumping-station with its phantom gunfire, long rows of canvas troughs had been run out, and from these the teams of dusty mules were drinking, six strung together, while their drivers, Cape-boys, with ribbons of giraffe hide in their hats, quarrelled for precedence. The phantom guns were never silent.

It was difficult to believe that so much life could suddenly have blossomed in that deserted place. One centre of unusual clamour was the tin shanty of Nazareth, the Goanese trader, whose stores have always followed our armies in this campaign. That night he was hard put to to deal with the rush of trade, and next day he had as little to show as a field that locusts have stripped. Night fell, and the camps of the Indian regiments were soon silent, but with the Rhodesians a very pleasant time began; for many of their old friends of the First Brigade came round to see them, and notably the Baluchis, a regiment with which there already

existed a strong bond of sentiment which dated
from the hard day of Salaita. In that engagement,
when the flanking movement of the South African
regiments had failed, it was the 130th Baluchis
who sustained the weight of German counter-attacks
which fell so heavily that for a time the regiment
was actually surrounded. Seeing this, the Rhodesia regiment, who were then in reserve, had asked
to be allowed to go to their help ; and though this
was never necessary, and the request refused, the
Baluchis did not forget. Next day, on parade, the
Indian officers of the regiment handed to their
Colonel a letter addressed to the Rhodesians. It
was written in the formal phrases of the *babu*, and
the grammar was not in every way perfect, but the
spirit of admiration and brotherhood in arms which
lay beneath it was a fine thing, and it was a fine
thing to have expressed it. Many months later, the
Rhodesians and the Baluchis were given the privilege of entering Morogoro together at the head of
the First Brigade.

Other visitors there were in this expectant camp.
For a moment I saw Bishop Furze of Pretoria, that
most militant Christian. He was going to attach
himself, he said, to Smuts's headquarters. ' If he 'll
have me,' he added, for he knew the General well,

and respected him for a strong man like himself.
'He fears neither God nor man,' he said, 'and
particularly the former.'

We lingered, long after the hour of the 'sun-
downer,' about the tent of old M—— the one-armed
elephant hunter, and there many friendships were
renewed. Here, too, came Cherry Kearton, the
photographer of big game, who had now been
attached to the Naval Air Service. He said that
he was going to fly to Tabora. Tabora ! . . . that
infinitely distant and unattainable capital, when
we had barely crossed the frontier. He had come
to ask M—— about the nature of the country on
those high plateaux, and it was strange that he
should have been able to ask a question about
Central Africa which M—— could not answer; but
seeing that this was the case there was nothing left
for Kearton to do but talk about himself, and the
old days when he had taken photographs of the
Masai spearing lions in the bush-veldt. And all
the time, beneath our light words, I think we were
conscious of the fact that we were on the edge of
something big ; that now, for the first time in
East Africa, we were coming to grips with the
enemy ; that it was going to be an invasion, a
conquest ; and that we were going to experience

emotions such as had fallen to few Englishmen in this war at that time.

So night fell upon us, and in a little while there was no sound in the camp of Taveta but the shrill cicala trills in the mud walls of the perimeter.

Next morning before dawn I was awakened by a sound with which later days made me very familiar, the noise of several thousand Indians hawking and scraping their throats, the ceremony with which their day is begun. Already our camp was astir, but there was little to do before we marched out : for our tents were left standing, as were those of the brigade at M'buyuni, for all the Germans on the Pare to see. It was a heavy morning with a low sky drooping from Kilimanjaro upon the forest lawns. For the most part we saw little even of these, for the bush pressed very close upon our track, so that we could not even be certain where our flankers were. It seemed strange that we must move with so much caution over a road which had been for several months in our hands ; but we had been warned against road mines, and in those parts the bush was so dense that a whole army might have lain in wait for us a few hundred yards from the road and never have been seen. In many places the bush was continuous for miles, but from time to time we came upon patches where it had thinned away, leaving long slades of waving grasses beyond which the hills could be seen. Very green and beautiful they were after the rains, with the richness of a giant meadow. I did not know then that they were features of great importance in this bush warfare, that they opened a field for maxim fire on troops emerging from the close bush, and that, indeed, a daring enemy might have made such use of them at any minute on that day.

Yet we saw nothing of the enemy nor even any sign of his more peaceful life in that day's trek, though we had imagined that these wide foothills of the great mountain were among his most fertile lands. Always the road ran westward across the valleys of a whole system of streams running to the Lumi or Pangani, the rivers of those parts. At every valley bottom there was a rough bridge, or else a sandy nullah, which delayed our transport; and in these valleys, suddenly, the character of the dry bush would change, and greater trees appear with a green foliage which contrasted with the bush-veldt's ashen silver: tall spathodeas with a fiery blossom, and shapeless baobabs. In some of these nullahs a trickle of water or a rock pool remained, and here we were at some trouble to keep our African stretcher-bearers in hand; for they think that it is a foolish thing for any man walking in Africa not to drink whenever he may, and we, on the other hand, were not anxious to make acquaintance with dysentery in a country where it might play the devil with us in a little time.

It was strange, we thought, that we saw no German plantations in this well-watered land, and stranger still that no native villages or isolated *bandas* were to be seen. Indeed, there was no sign of human life in all this bush but one, and to that there clung, in a strange degree, the peculiarly sinister atmosphere which sometimes attaches itself to material objects which have once been associated with the activities of man and have then been left behind in some lonely place. From time to time we saw bee-hives, shaped like long and narrow barrels and made from tree trunks hollowed by fire, hanging in the topmost branches of the greater trees in the bush, a lure for the swarms of wild bees that gather aromatic honey from the flowers of the brushwood. It was strange to see these rotting pieces of man's handicraft in that very solitary place. As we walked, a man who had fought at Tanga, in the first disastrous assault from the sea, told me how the outlying bush through which our men had passed had been full of these hives, and how the Germans had snared the pathways of the wood with cords which set them in motion, so that when our attack began the hives were roused, and the wild bees swarmed in their millions, doing more damage to one Indian regiment than the German maxims.

So we marched on into the heat of the day. About noon the sun began to beat heavily upon us, and our progress became a torment; for the surface of this earth road had become so worn by motor-lorry convoys moving into the conquered territory that the marching troops, and the mules of the Rhodesian machine-guns, which were in front of me, churned up dust into the air which blackened our dry lips.

At length, in the early afternoon, we came to a greater valley than any we had met before, by which the river Himo carries the icy waters of Kilimanjaro to the Pangani. On a high brow a mile or so beyond this river we camped for the night. It was a beautiful open hillside, from which the bush had been cleared; from there we overlooked the whole wide valley of the Pangani, bounded by the Pare Hills. A richly wooded and a green country it seemed, and one worth fighting for.

When we marched in, all that green hilltop was scattered with many dwarf flowers, blooming there in different and delicate hues, which resembled the upright mountain centaury at home. They had sprung afresh after the falling of the rains, and the feet of our army trampled them to death in thousands, but they were so beautiful that I must always remember them. We bivouacked, and soon the smell of cooking was in the air, the fumes of wood smoke from our own fires, and from the Indian lines the slightly rancid odour of burning ghee with which they browned their *chapattis* of *atta*.

A wonderful night beneath misty stars. Over the lands beneath us the Southern Cross hung, as though it were pointing the path of our invasion. Poised amid milky nebulae it hung, and as the labouring earth rolled over, swung, as a ship swings with the change of tide.

CHAPTER III

NEXT morning we were off at dawn. For many miles we marched within the same green walls. They lay so close together that the churned dust of our column became imprisoned between them, blinding us as we went. Still there was no sign of habitation. We passed many dry watercourses, and all the time the road was dropping gently from the high land about Kilimanjaro towards the plain. One could appreciate the change of altitude even in that dusty air, which became staler as we descended, and mingled curiously with the aromatic odour of trampled brushwood. Among the flowers of these dwarf shrubs many quick butterflies hovered, fluttering restlessly about them as we passed. In the depths of the bush melancholy hornbills called to one another.

At length we came, in the heat of the day, to a place where the road widened and the red earth gave way to a black dust like powdered peat in which our transport animals floundered. The character of the bush changed at the same time; the endless thorn-trees thinned away, and in their place tall raffia palms arose from a tangled undergrowth, making a picture nearer to the conventional idea of tropical Africa than any we had seen. Not only the central road but many subsidiary tracks had been deeply worn by wheeled traffic, so that we guessed that we were approaching the site of some concentration. Many motor-cars with box bodies passed us, raising so much black dust that we were smothered with it. And a little later we found the clearing wider still, and that we were marching beside the new military railway which the Indian sappers had built from Voi to the Tanga line. In this open place lay a little dump of stores. A corporal of the A.S.C. sat beside them, and surveyed us as nonchalantly as if the passage of an invading division were the sort of thing that happened to him every day.

This, we were told, was the place which had been known as Store, and was, indeed, a depot of some importance. The way in which it came by its name was typical of that in which the operations of war thrust into sudden prominence places or natural features which would otherwise never have been known. A little Indian shop, marked on the German Survey maps, had been the origin of *Store*; just as the wooden bridge across the Pangani near

Tanda Station, for which a fortnight later we were to fight, gave rise to the name of *German Bridge*, for a long time our railhead on the Tanga line; and a small group of raffia trees upon the right bank of the Pangani below Buiko became *Palms*, an important camping place and aerodrome. These names were so often on men's tongues that the small significance of the places themselves came as something of a shock. I had often heard our men talking of Store. Well, this was Store : a dump of biscuit boxes and a corporal of the A.S.C.

Over that black desert of dust we marched on, the swamp of raffia palms on either side, until I saw something in the long grass which explained, perhaps, the reason why Store had been remembered in the minds of men—a little group of graves, with white crosses over them, in which were buried those who fell in the action which followed the taking of the Latema-Reata crest.

As we passed I could see the names which were carved upon them, and knew that they numbered many men of our own regiment. In a little while, again, we saw the shallow rifle-pits from which they had fought in that action, and here our men began to talk, remembering many incidents of the day.

By this time we were near our journey's end;
for the wide road suddenly debouched upon an
open space of flat land, lying in the apex of the
triangle formed by the confluence of the Ruwu
river and the Soko Nassai, a plain of coarse grasses
over which our men had advanced a few weeks
before beneath a sheet of maxim fire. In this
grassy place, scattered with the rusty fragments of
the German shells, it had been decided that the
army of invasion should encamp. Already a single
regiment, the 29th Punjabis, awaited us there. We
could see their blue-and-yellow flag ahead of us.

In that open camp of Soko Nassai, as it was
called, the heat was terrific. No tree of any kind
mitigated the sun's power, and the sight of green
forest trees down by the river and the cool summits
of the Pare did nothing but emphasise the glare.
We of the Rhodesian Regiment encamped there in
the open, as best we could, with no shelter but that
of our ground-sheets between us and the sun and
no inclination to go further in the heat in search of
protection. But the men of the 130th Baluchis,
who were camped next to us, were soon astir and
trooping down to the riverside, where they cut for
themselves branches and wide fans of the palms
which grow in watery places. These they carried

The Sepoys bathed their brown bodies in the shade.

back to the open ground and made themselves green
bowers: and their *bhistis* came home staggering
under great leather *chhagals* of water from the
Pangani, with which the sepoys bathed their brown
bodies in the shade, and looked far cooler than all
the rest of our dusty cavalcade. They were fine
fellows, these men of the 130th, frontiersmen, lean
and lithe and of a splendid physique, and later I
learned that I need not wish to be in a tight corner
with better men. When the night fell with a hint
of river coldness in the air, the bowers which they
had built themselves were full of chatter as an
autumn reed-bed in which the whirling cohorts of
starlings have settled, till, at last, they hushed, as
suddenly. From their lines there came no sound
except the falsetto singing of some Pathan minstrel.
He sang the song, 'Zakhmi Del'—the wounded
heart—which all Pathans love, and when he had
finished there was absolute silence.

In the Rhodesian Headquarters we sat late over
our fire. Next day the real business was to begin.
We knew very well that of those who were gathered
in the firelight many would not return; but we
were equally certain that when the end came we
should have conquered German East. Capell, the
Colonel, was very sanguine. 'Two months will do

it,' he said, and I think that most of us believed him. But M——, the old elephant hunter, shook his head.

' I wish I could agree with you,' he said. ' Still we can only do our duty.'

Doing one's duty is not a thing one talks about, and yet on the lips of this man of many wars it seemed a natural thing to have said ; and as for his doubts, there was no man in that camp who knew the country better.

This was the problem by which we were faced :

By the beginning of the rains the whole of the Kilimanjaro area had been cleared of the enemy, while the Tanga line had been taken as far south as the station, above which we were now encamped, though the crests of the Pare Mountains, which overlooked our present position, were still in the enemy's hands. To the west, a South African division under Van Deventer had reached out by forced marches to Kondoa Irangi, a settlement of some importance, from which the enemy's ad-ministrative capital Tabora was threatened, and with it the continuity of the Central Railway. In the Pare Mountains, however, and in all the length of the Tanga line, the Germans were very firmly established. They were well provisioned ; the last blockade runner had replenished their stores of ammunition ; at their back they had the fertile highlands of the Usambara, and in the Tanga railway itself a swift and easy line of communication or retreat.

Our first task, then, was to expel the Germans from the Pare and the Usambara, and to gain control of the Tanga line.

To advance in force through that wide tangle of mountains was impossible. To push back the enemy along his railway by frontal pressure would be nearly as hard, for he had the advantage of us in communications, and, for all we knew, in machine-guns and artillery, and had prepared positions with his accustomed skill at many points of advantage on the line. Such, we knew, was Lembeni, where the railway makes a curve into the hills which can be enfiladed in all its length. Such, again, was Same, where the line cuts in between the masses of the Pare and the little hill of Kitamulu. And, more important than any of these, such was the bottle neck of Mikocheni, where the Pangani, a swift river and unbridged which protects the Tanga line in all its course, swirls in to the very foot of the Pare. At any one of these places the enemy might stand with everything in his favour.

There remained one alternative : a flanking move down the left bank of the Pangani which protected his southern face; and this was not an adventure which might be lightly undertaken. In the first place, the country through which it would carry us was largely unexplored, and there was no knowing what natural difficulties we might encounter. For part of our course it was certain that we must hack our way through virgin bush. In the second place, the valley of the Pangani had already acquired a most sinister reputation for disease. We might look to lose a great number of men through sickness ; we might look to lose a great part of the transport on which the existence of the force depended through horse-sickness and tsetse-fly. Again, for a move of this kind to be wholly successful it would be necessary for our column, fighting its way with bullock transport through a savage land, to move rather faster than the enemy, who had at his disposal an intact railway system with plenty of rolling stock. In that unlikely event a part of his forces might be surrounded. To be partially successful, our advance must be so swift that he must be forced to retire at an uncomfortable rate, or even compelled to choose between a rearguard action and disaster. If this were achieved there were, as we have already seen, several places of election at which he might make his stand.   And this was the best that we hoped for.

The flanking march down the Pangani was the one which the strategy of Smuts dictated, and its performance was entrusted to the First East African Division, a force of which the units had already proved their worth not only in the infinitely trying months of our long defensive, but in the battles for Kilimanjaro earlier in the year.   While the bulk of the First Division moved down the Pangani by forced marches, it was decided that its Second Brigade, under General Hannyngton, should press directly down the Tanga line, while a third mobile column, consisting mainly of the King's African Rifles, struck across from M'buyuni, past Lake Jipe to either the N'gulu or the Gonya gap, the only passes in the unbroken chain of the Pare Mountains, and threatened the enemy's rear if he had not, by that time, evacuated the railway as far south as Same.

Such was the position when we lay waiting that night in the camp of Soko Nassai.   The units which were to be engaged in this adventure were as follows :   the First East African Brigade under General Sheppard, consisting of the 2nd Rhodesia

Regiment (Colonel Essex Capell), the 130th Baluchis
(Colonel Dyke), the 2nd Kashmere Rifles (Colonel
Lyall), and the 29th Punjabis (Major James), to
which were added a company of the 61st Pioneers,
a section of the 27th Mountain Battery—the 5th
and 6th Batteries of South African Field Artillery,
and a squadron of the 17th Cavalry.   Other units
under the divisional command of General Hoskins
were : the 25th Royal Fusiliers (Colonel Driscoll) ;
the East African Mounted Rifles, a corps locally
raised ; the machine-gun section and Mounted
Infantry of the Loyal North Lancs, and a Cornwall
(Territorial) Howitzer Battery.   With the Divisional
troops moved also Sir John Willoughby's Armoured
Cars, the 'Z' Signalling Company, and a wireless
section.   Attached to the division, but acting under
the orders of the Commander-in-Chief, were the 5th
and 6th South African Infantry, under General
Beves, which were known as the Force Reserve.
These were the troops which lay camped at Soko
Nassai on 22nd May 1916.   In three months' time
they had not only freed the Tanga line of a stub-
born enemy, but had swept through the heart of
a savage and waterless country and struck again at
the Central Railway, isolating the capital, Dar-es-
Salaam.   I do not think that so great a military

movement had ever been made before through the heart of tropical Africa. It is certain that the men who were engaged in it endured with a wonderful patience hardships which were unequalled in any other campaign, lacking, perforce, in food and even water, marching day after day without respite beneath a vertical sun, ravaged by diseases from which there was no escape in a country which even the natives of Africa had found to be incompatible with human life.

CHAPTER IV

AT moonrise on the 23rd of May, the First Brigade moved out from Soko Nassai, that ancient market. At eleven o'clock precisely the advance-guard passed the red lamp of the Brigade Headquarters. Very quietly we moved on our way: for though the shadowy hill named Baumann Kop in front of us was in our hands, the enemy's scouts have an easy time in such thick country, and any great disturbance would have robbed our advance of the feature of surprise.

At the confluence of the two rivers lay a great tangle of creeks and reedy backwaters which had been spanned by trestle bridges, a whole series of them, guarded on either side by a palisade of grasses to shield the eyes of mules and oxen from the terrifying sight of water. Perhaps the darkness aided us in this: for the moon was yet low and the night very dense, being thicker for the moisture of the swampy air. Over these bridges we marched slowly, as though the animals were feeling their way in the dark, and with very little noise except when hoofs stumbled on the wooden corduroy of the track, or the A.T. carts heavily jolted. Below all these sounds, and almost part of the night's silence, the whistling of many thousand frogs filled an air which smelt faintly mephitic. Over the marshes fireflies flickered. It was a most beautiful night.

The uncertain footing of our transport animals in the neighbourhood of the bridges was not by any means the only reason for our delay : for, in a very little while, we had come to a part of the ancient trading track which was unknown to any but our intelligence officers, and to them imperfectly, while it seemed not unlikely that the enemy might have got wind of our progress and at least attempt to harass us. Therefore, our advance-guard and their flankers moved with the utmost caution, and from time to time long halts were called, in which we were at liberty to wonder what had happened. When, at last, the first uncertainties of the march were over, we settled down to a steady pace of rather embarrassing slowness, somewhere between two and three miles an hour, but nearer two, which, though it may have been heaven for a laden ox, was infinitely tiring for a man.

We shuffled along in silence over the dust with

D

which our advance-guard felted the road. There was neither speech nor light to break the monotony of our progress, for both talking and smoking were forbidden : 'one heard only the slow—intolerably slow—drag of many feet, the creaking of the harness in the mules' packs, or perhaps the clink of a loose chain. Out of this uneven concert of sounds a sort of rhythm emerged when once the column was fairly going. It took its measure with me, sitting almost asleep in the saddle, from the slow lunge of my horse's walk, and fitted itself, I cannot tell why, to the words of a hymn which were gradually evoked from some storehouse of my childhood. They ran, as I have said, very slowly. They were dragged with long pauses between each note, as sometimes a village congregation will sing them.

> Time . like . an . ev . er . roll . ing . stream
> Bears . all . its . sons . a . way ;
> They . die . for . got . ten . as . a . dream
> Dies . at . the . ope . ning . day.

And then, in revolt at the crudity of this rhythmical pattern and the torture to which the indifferent words were put in its maintenance, I would start fitting them with their proper accentuation and liberty of phrasing above the insistent pattern, and it gave me a little satisfaction to free the poor things from their bondage . . . they even got for themselves a certain dignity which I hadn't suspected. I wondered who wrote them, and thought of the immortality which is assured through I know not what hoarding of the childish memory to those who write the hymns which children sing, without thinking, in church.

Still we moved on through the dark. It was difficult to guess where we were, for once we had left the twinkling signal light on Baumann's Hill there was no landmark in all that flat valley of the Pangani. And really, in the sleepiness induced by our rhythmical progress, one might easily have imagined oneself in a country far different— even, without any great effort, in England. For in this soft darkness, with its faint river chill and its misty moonlight, the thorns of the African bush did not differ greatly in contour from our English hawthorn in places where it is writhen by wind or tangled with great age. Even the coarse grass and the small shrubs at our feet might well have passed for a rough pasture ; and the greater trees, which stood some way back from the edge of the bush, bordering long slades, were too distant to be recognised, so that the thorned mimosa might well have been taken for the gentle birch and even the ugliness of the baobab be hidden. A field path in roughish country on a summer night. . . .

Only one thing was there to dissuade us from this illusion, and that was ever present in our nostrils: the aromatic odour of the dwarf scrub, which with its dusty purple flowers spreads all over this inhospitable heart of Africa, and was here so trodden and bruised that the air was saturate with the perfume of its essential oils. A not unpleasant scent I thought it on that night. Now it will speak to me for ever of desolation and dust, recalling, by a most intimate association, the other mingled smells of iodine and blood.

At five o'clock in the morning the shapes of all the trees grew more distinct. We saw, for the first time, the tawny colour of the dust with which we were powdered, and the bruised herbs in the track beneath our feet. Gone, too, was all illusion. For this was Africa, stark and savage: not merely German East, but all the central waste from Rhodesia to Somaliland, that waterless bush where man is a stranger, where nothing but curiosity or lust for the blood of big game need ever take him. With sunrise we had gained upon a more open steppe: wide stretches of red sand spilled upon a sloping land. The sun rose triumphantly, as though he were conscious of the intolerable strength which would enable him to climb to the very centre of the sky in the space of six hours—it has been said before and incomparably : ' rejoicing as a giant to run his course.' But here, where the sky was cloudless and bordered by the black rim of the Pare, over which he lifted, one was particularly conscious of his titanic energy. So must he have risen, I thought, upon the first dawn of the world, before ever there was an astronomer to find spots on his face, or a philosopher to question the eternity of his dominion.

To us, who were shortly to suffer beneath his power, the sunrise gave new life. Straightway our retarded pace became less tiring. In a little while the Kavirondo stretcher-bearers who marched before me began to chatter. And indeed they were like boys released from school, for they fear the dark, and silence is most unnatural to them. When they march at night they huddle close together for the sake of a little fortuitous courage ; but they are by nature a happy people, cheerful under the most distressing physical conditions, and with the fear of darkness no longer brooding over them they soon began to straggle over the track. The harsh fumes

of native tobacco rose in the air, and I wondered
how they had got their light until I turned and saw
that one of them was carrying in the cup of his
hands the dry centre of a mealie cob. With this
slow burning tinder he had nursed a smouldering
fire all night, and the sight of him brought swiftly
to my mind the Promethean legend and the Titan's
hollow stick of fennel, so that in this chill dawn I
seemed again to be riding in the dawn of the world :
and indeed this land was as unvexed by man as any
Thracian wild and the people as simple as those to
whom the son of Zeus brought fire.

So the sun lifted clear of the jagged outline of
the Pare. We had come to another of those expanses of sandy open ground, rising, in this case,
to a crest from which there swept down to meet it
a meadow (as one might say) of tall grasses, washed
in the horizontal gold. With the daylight a warm
breeze moved up from the south, sweeping these
grasses into fields of waving light. A bird, I think
it was a rainbird, sang a short song of almost
northern tenderness. It was difficult to believe
that we were marching only a little south of the
Equator—more difficult still to realise that we were
at war ; that within a moment the waving edge of
grasses might crackle into fire. The idea was alto-

gether incongruous: that we should go trampling
through this land, in a cavalcade that bristled with
instruments of destruction, marching south into a
warm breeze with fields of rippling light and a
golden sunrise on our left.

At last we came to a thin belt of forest, and
heard above the silky sound of the stirred grasses
the rushing noise of a rapid river. We had reached
the bank of the Pangani, the stream with which
we must keep company so long. I cantered over
to the bank, and saw a race of water no wider than
the Lumi, tawny and swift. All through the rest
of that morning the river was near us, and as the
day wore on and the sun mounted higher, the water
was good to think on, being the only cool thing in
all that burning land.

Early in the afternoon, having reached another
of those open stretches of the steppe which seem to
have been made for camping-grounds, we formed a
perimeter, with the Pangani—our most precious
water—on one side, and on the other a low ridge
from the top of which an expanse of bush (which
we should have called impenetrable until we realised
how bush could be dealt with) spread like a dark
sea, moulded in many wavelike convolutions, until
it broke upon the foothills of the Pare. All that day

we had seen no enemy. More than this : we had seen no sign of human habitation. An extraordinary thing this seemed to us who had marched through that country in the golden morning and had found it fair. We did not realise then what was borne in on us so heavily in later days : that the Pangani levels, for all their beauty—for all their bright skies, their golden grasses, and the warm south wind that blows over them all day, were among the most pestilential regions in all Africa. That is why the Masai, those great herdsmen, have left the grasslands beside the stream unpastured, and why, that day and for many days to come, we saw not so much as a single hut of reeds, far less a village.

Next day the Rhodesia Regiment was to form the advance-guard, and we expected to meet the enemy. Soon after dark there came to us a tallish fellow, of a slight figure. He looked at the same time anxious and very ill, with thin nervous features and sunken eyes. One gathered that he had reasons for this appearance. Two days before he had made his way to the Pangani rapids, where there is a passage of the river, and found there an enemy company encamped. What is more he had had the bad luck to be discovered and at last surrounded.

'It was a near thing,' he said, laughing. He laughed, but there was still a hunted look in his eyes. 'And they're there now if you want them,' he said.

He still showed traces of this rough experience in a torn cheek, and, I imagined, in that strangely fragile appearance.

He left us, and next there came an officer of the Indian Cavalry to talk with the Colonel of the morrow's work. The idea of these operations was simple enough : to detach the enemy force at the rapids, a single company, we were told, from their friends on the Tanga railway. It was true that they might escape to the west of the Pangani by means of the footbridge above the rapids; but that wouldn't really matter as long as they did not rejoin the main body.

'I see . . .' said the officer of the 17th; 'you want us to engage them and hold them ? '

'Well, that's the idea,' said Capell, smiling.

No more was said. We all turned in early, for we were to start at dawn. I slept under a tarpaulin which old M—— had slung between two A.T. carts. As long as we were awake we could hear the soft breathing of the bullocks, who lay down near their shafts; and once, a little after midnight, the pro-

longed boom of a distant explosion. We knew at
once that it must be the railway bridge beyond
Lembeni that the Germans were destroying, and
from this we guessed that the enemy must be aware
that our turning movement had begun.

CHAPTER V

NEXT morning at two o'clock we moved off again through the same aromatic dusk, and, after the sun had risen, the same golden morning. Now we were never far from the Pangani; not that we ever saw its waters, for these were hidden by the graceful masses of acacia which lined the banks; but sometimes we heard the river's voice, a deep note, upon the surface of which the thin murmur of a grass country in sunshine floated lightly; and even when we did not hear, the darkness of that slender forest belt marked the course of the stream.

Sunrise found us crossing yet another of those open plains, in later days too rare, where the river had overspilled itself in the rainy season, flooding a number of shallow sandy pools   With the passing of the floods these pools had dried, leaving a plastic surface upon which were now imprinted, set and hardened by the baking sun, the footprints of all the forest beasts which had come there for watering. In one small patch of sand I counted the spoor of lion, leopard, waterbuck, and rhinoceros; while the whole plain was printed with the light hoof-marks of the lesser kinds of buck. In another place, in which, I suppose, the ground had been more yielding, one could see where a great buffalo had struggled to free himself from the mire in the imprint of two trampling hoofs planted close together, and along the edge of the river wallowing hippopotami had sunk great pits.

Indeed this country must have been full of game, though we saw little of it. Once, a fine bull oryx found himself cut off from his home in the bush by our far-winding column. Time after time he galloped up to the line, turning when he came face to face with us; and when he had tried three or four places he pulled all his noble courage together, charging a thin line of machine-gun porters, who gave before his straight horns so that he escaped, followed by our cheers.

No words can tell the golden loveliness of those early mornings by the Pangani, where neither man nor beast can live: always, beneath a sky of strangely temperate blue, tall grasses waving in a warm wind from the south. So it was in their early hours, and for a little while before their sudden sunset; but in the middle of the day, when there was no shelter from the vertical sun, the air above the sandy flats swam with heat, and the dust from our moving cavalcade dried upon our faces and parched our lips. I think that we felt the heat less than did our cattle, and particularly the bullocks which swayed, panting, with a look of distress in their patient eyes whenever we crossed those sandy patches in which the wheels of the A.T. carts sank. But this was a trek in which neither man nor beast could be spared. All of us, struggling through sand-drifts, hacking our way through the dry bush, were matched against a well-laid railway with plenty of rolling stock. The explosions in the night had encouraged us; we guessed that the Germans were on the move, and knew why we were being hurried forward through the heat of the day.

A little after midday, when we had been marching for twelve hours, a halt was called. For some time we had been advancing very slowly through the bush, and we knew that we could not now be very far from those rapids by which Pretorius had told us the enemy were posted. We gathered that our advance-guard were even now getting into touch with them, that the cavalry might already be between them and their friends. And then, as we moved on and at length emerged from the bush, a sight most unexpected met our eyes. Here lay another of those wide, sandy expanses, but far

greater than any we had seen. In the midst of it
a pair of small lakes fringed with reeds : and
straight before us, set across our path, a square
elevation shaped like a fort or a low house, a most
sinister sight in that flat plain. We could not think
what to make of it. A machine-gun posted on its
crown could have swept all the open ground over
which we were advancing. We halted a mile or so
away, and watched it to see what would happen;
but our glasses showed us that the cavalry were
already past it and were not very far from where
the line of the Rhodesian advance-guard was moving
forward. In a little while we too advanced.

This strange four-square outcrop of rock was
named in the German maps Njumba-ya-Mawe : the
House of Stone. Our slow column filed between
it and the reeded pools. This was the first open
space which could contain the whole of it, and
ours the first invasion of such magnitude that had
ever broken in upon that solitary place. From the
summit of the House of Stone the General watched
us move past. A peculiarly vivid picture the place
must have shown him of tawny sands, green reed-
beds, bounded by the edge of grey-green bush and
the tender sky. As we passed the pools, a flight
of white egrets rose in the sunny air and beat their

wings above us. We were ordered to halt. One
would have thought—once forgetting that we had
been on the march for twelve hours—that the whole
affair was in the nature of a picnic.

Why were we halting? Where were the enemy
who had held the position near the rapids? In a
few moments we learned what had happened, for
our disappointed advance-guard came in. They
had been only a little too late, seeing the enemies'
dust almost within range, but the squadron of
cavalry, who found themselves at this critical
moment only a little in the rear of the advancing
Rhodesians, concluded that in the bush the enemy
were certain to escape, and so decided it was not
worth while following them. It was not long before
we realised that these sowars, with their handsome
Pathan faces and their well-groomed horses, could
not operate successfully in the dense bush. It
chanced that later in the campaign they were particularly unlucky in the matter of casualties ; indeed
they lost more in proportion than any other regiment, and in passing any judgment upon them one
must remember that this was no country for cavalry
manœuvres, and that the South African Mounted
Brigade were equally unsuccessful.

After an hour's halt in the sun we started off

once more.   At this point in its course the Pangani
makes a slight curve to westward about the bases
of low hills covered in bush—' thin bush,' said the
German maps—and these hills lay ahead of us.
Now more than ever, since the force at the rapids
had escaped, it was important that we should move
quickly, and so the 61st Pioneers and the 2nd Kashmiris went ahead of us to cut with their *kukris* a
way through the ' thin bush ' and make a road
more direct than the old trading track which, from
what we knew of it in the past, was as likely as not to
be clogged with bush which was by no means thin.
So we soon found ourselves climbing slowly a rough
path thick set with the twisted roots of thorn and
torn stumps which the Pioneers had left.   In some
places the road was very steep, too steep as I
thought, to take our wheeled transport, and the more
so because our oxen were already tired out.   But
we had it from Pretorius, who was said to know
the country, that the thick bush only lasted for
another four miles, and that after that an easy trek
would bring us to the water for which our beasts
were fainting.

For a mile or so we moved slowly up the slope.
This bush was not greatly unlike any other patch
of dense undergrowth within a hundred miles ; the

same twisted shapes of multitudinous thorns, the same tangles of lush cactus and chevaux-de-frise of wild sisal, with now and then a dry candelabra-tree lifting its symmetrical branches over all. And the thickets, as usual, were strangely interspersed with lacunae where no green of any kind grew ; so that one was always on the point of thinking that one's troubles were over and the bush at an end.

Slowly we advanced another mile with many weary checks, and then another. Pretorius's four miles had already been covered. We could not count on more than two hours of daylight. The bush in front of us lay thicker than ever, and the Pioneers, however brave their spirits, had now been on the march for over sixteen hours. The advance-guard, pushing on for miles still and coming at length to the crown of that low hill-country, could only tell us that the bush seemed without end, stretching unbroken between the river and the mountains, and that there was no water in front of us. Anxious people with little to say rode to and fro along the length of the halted column. There was nothing to be known except that the bush grew thicker ahead, and that it was swarming with tsetse-fly.

' Keep your horses and mules in the open, away

E

from the trees.' A counsel of perfection : for the trees and the fly were everywhere.

Another hour passed. Under the shadow of the rise, the sweet wind that had moved all day from the south failed us. Some stink-ants had been disturbed, and to the hot aromatic smell of trampled shrubs was added another odour like that of dead horses. All around the bush was strangely silent. No bird was singing but one : the lesser hornbill, that spirit of dry places. From either side of the road they called to each other in hollow melancholy tones : a single note long sustained and followed by a number of shorter sounds, minutely flattening in tone until they reached a full semitone below the first. I think the note of this bird expresses more nearly the unutterable sadness of these waterless wastes of thorn than any other sound or scent or sight. Whenever its hollow melancholy note is heard, as homeless as a lost echo, there is no place for man, nor any joy in which he delights. This was the only sound we heard—and it seemed to mock our baulked progress—upon that dry hillside, unless it were the restless movements of our mules trying to shake the flies from their quarters and lashing their thick tails.

We, like the beasts, were faint with hunger and

. . . the Kashmiris . . . smothered us with a new layer of red dust (*p.* 57)

heat, and it came to us as a great relief when the Kashmiris—Dogras and Gurkhas—with little emotion showing on their wide Mongol faces, marched back again and smothered us with a new layer of red dust. The Pioneers, we were told, could do no more ; for in addition to the cruel density of the bush they had found the top of the hills scarred with innumerable nullahs, the stony beds of winter watercourses, each of which must be bridged over before our carts and wagons could move on. The order had been given to retire, and all of us were thankful. It is difficult always to remember that our forced marches were made, generally without food, within a few miles of the Equator.

But no sooner had I loaded my pack-mules and inspanned my bullocks, even before the dust of the passing Kashmiris had cleared away, than we heard rapid hoofs ascending the track, and three horsemen pushed by. The first I saw was a staff-officer with a brown pointed beard, who looked like a Dutchman. The third a young man of the kind who often wears a red hat. But the second was of a very different type : a man of heavy build with nothing of the exquisite in his carriage or attire. He wore a cord tunic which contrasted with the light drill of his companions, and his features were

in keeping with the rest of his appearance, rather
hard and coarse, with most masterful eyes : the
face of a man who is determined on success. I
recognised him at once, for a few months before in
Adderley Street, Capetown, I had seen a gigantic
poster, an imitation of those which put us to shame
in England a little earlier, bearing a signature and
the legend JOHN SMUTS WANTS YOU. But the man
whose horse now climbed our track seemed of a
stronger and coarser fibre than his picture. In his
swift passage one realised with an extraordinary
clearness the driving force that was behind all this
dusty pageantry of ours plodding through the centre
of Africa.

He had not been gone five minutes when the order
came back to us to advance. Wheeled transport
was to be left behind, but, for all that, the brigade
must move on. Fifteen hours of marching had
made us tired, and yet I do not think there was a
man in the brigade who was not cheered and
stimulated by this order. If we had been forced
to retire after all our fruitless waiting in the hot
bush our weariness would have told on us, and we
should have felt that the country had beaten us,
even though there were no shame in being beaten
by such a country.

This early token of the spirit of our higher command was actually more cheering to us than the prospect of food or rest. I think that in an adventure of this kind nothing could be more fatal to the morale of troops than to be spared hunger or fatigue in the face of difficulties.

So we moved on, curiously lightened in spirit, and actually at an easier pace, for we had shed our lumbering transport so that, for the first time, a man could stretch his legs. All the thick bush through which we passed was floored with a loose sandy soil which rose in dense clouds, filling our eyes and blackening our parched lips. The pioneers' road twisted interminably between the hacked tree-stumps : for the shortest way of penetrating bush of this kind is to take a rough bearing and, carrying this in mind, to follow the line of least resistance. The turning of the column and the retirement of the Kashmiris had somewhat deranged our marching order, and I found myself and my stretcher-bearers plodding through the dust of the 27th Mountain Battery mules. These splendid creatures walked at a great pace in spite of their heavy loads, too fast indeed for my small Somali animals with their panniers and *pakhals* of sweet water, so that in the end my transport lagged behind, with a corporal in charge, leaving me and my bearers alone. I had known already something of the dust of Africa; but that which rose from this new earthen road and those sandy nullahs, first trampled by the feet of the brigade, and then churned into clouds by the hoofs of the battery mules, was as dense as those gyrating dust-devils which sometimes sweep the dry veldt. The thick walls of bush on either side prisoned the air, and our smarting eyes could scarcely see the unit next in front of us.

For two hours we marched at a great pace, and by that time we had reached the gravelly summit of those hills. At a small clearing we halted, and in the fading light saw nothing but a sea of stunted tree-tops, stretching on every side, bounded towards the east by the darkening masses of the Pare, to the west by the flat skyline of the Lossogonoi Plateau beyond the river, and the whole roofed by a lurid sky in which the western mountains shone like beaten copper. Somewhere beyond that line of hills lay Kondoa Irangi, and the division of Van Deventer.

We would gladly have bivouacked where we halted, but there was no water. At any rate it was encouraging to know that the Pangani lay between us and those hills. We fell in again in the darkness, and now the dust did not seem quite so trouble-some. My stretcher-bearers kept close together and were silent ; but from the narrowness of the way our column was now greatly extended, the whole brigade moving in single file. The night was very dark, for the moon had not yet risen, and in a little while one developed a sort of fifth sense which told one instinctively where to avoid the trailing thorn or the torn tree-stump. There was no noise at all except the shuffle of our feet : so that when some great beast went crashing through the thickets we wondered what had happened. And, indeed, an enemy who knew where we were going could have made short work of us with a couple of maxims ; but we chose our way as we made it, and the light of the next day showed us that we had steered rather an eccentric course.

For two more hours we marched, and then, with a sense of the most profound relief, we found that we were going downhill once more. Another hour— and the bush became sensibly thinner. At the end of the next a cloudy moon had risen. We were passing through a narrow way between grasses as high as a man's shoulder, and this change from the alien atmosphere of the bush was subtly reassuring, as though we had really stumbled into some pathway cutting a moonlit cornfield at home. We halted many times, resting our bodies on the stubbly ground, and in one of these halts a strange sound came to us, very like the silky note of a cornfield waving in the wind ; but the grasses among which we lay were motionless, and no wind stirred. And then it came to me suddenly that the sound should have been more welcome, for it was that of the swift Pangani half deadened by its forest curtain.

Then there came another sound, a high metallic note, many times repeated, not unlike that of some tropical birds ; and as we passed from the region of high grasses to what illusion would have painted for me as water-meadows, a red lantern swung in the dark, and the voice of the Brigadier, as sanguine as ever, called to me :

' Who are you ? '

' M.O. Rhodesians, sir.'

' Oh, is that you, Doctor ? . . . Go straight ahead, as quickly as you can. This is a beastly place, full of fly and mosquitoes, but we must make the best of it.' His cheerfulness was worth a lot to us that night as on many others.

And now I saw that the metallic note which I had mistaken for the song of a bird proceeded from the hammering in of many steel pegs to which the maxim mules were to be tethered. Under a great tree, not far from the riverside, the Rhodesian Headquarters were settled. A fire had been lighted, but its flames were not strong enough to illumine the tops of the great trees above' us. Around the fire the high grass had been trampled down, and leaning there against my saddle after a mouthful of the Colonel's whisky, a sweet sense of physical tiredness stole through my limbs, so sweet that I do not think anything in the world could have disordered my content.

At the same time the oozy ground from which the grasses were growing was very cold and damp. I knew, well enough, that it might leave the elder of us with a legacy of lumbago, and so I suggested that I should send over for a couple of stretchers, on which the Colonel and the second in command might spend the night. Colonel Capell's eye had a cold gleam in it, and he smiled slightly, as he often does when there is trouble ahead. He said, ' You haven't stretchers enough for the whole regiment, have you ? Well then, we 'll do without them.'

Of course, it was sheer perversity, but perversity of a very admirable kind. It was the same spirit (*panache*, if you will) which kept the Rhodesians in the shell-swept camp at M'siha, because ' it wasn't worth moving when they 'd just comfortably settled down.' A fine soldier and a gallant gentleman all the same.

A fine soldier and a gallant gentleman all the same (p. 64)

CHAPTER VI

IN that camp by the river sleep did not come easily. I suppose we were too tired to sleep. I lay there staring at the fire, where the wood embers were gradually falling to white ash, and listening to the restlessness of the night where so much life moved by the river. The Colonel's orderly threw another bough on the fire. The boiling sap hissed with a sound that was wholly proper to the night, and then the bark cracked and broke into flame, lighting the figures of the men who lay about our fire, and I fell to wondering what manner of men we really were whom a blind fate had dumped down together in a spot where no man had ever trodden before.

I saw the Colonel lying there, glowing within, as I made sure, from the consciousness of the stretcher's rejection, and rather enjoying that cold couch in his rôle of old campaigner. Further off lay M——, who now for many years had scarcely slept beneath any roof but that velvety sky in which the Southern Cross is hung ; and beyond him B—— the Quarter-master, already fast asleep. Then the fire flickered

on to the spare face of Capell's orderly, a lanky
fellow who had fought in all the wars of Africa,
and once—how many years ago ?—had been at
Rugby School. I could not help wondering what
all these men were thinking of ; and then, strangely
enough, the sight of each of them impressed me
with a sudden memory of the places with which
they were connected in my mind : so that when I
thought of the Colonel I saw those homely fields
that lie beneath the Lickey Hills, and the great
lake at Cofton, swarming with winter wild-fowl.
The dim form of M—— gave me a vision of the
mountains of Skye, rising black over a grey-green
sea ; while from B——, most precious memory of
all, I stole a dream of the turf moors of Somerset,
golden in buttercup time, and yet another of stone-
walled farmyards in autumn, with the taste of
pomace in the air, and white mists lapping the
lower cliffs of Mendip. So, numbering remembered joys, I snatched what sleep the mosquitoes
would allow me.

I must have been sleeping lightly, for a sudden
cry in the night made me hold my breath and then
the darkness was full of confused sound : with the
shouts of men, the trampling of mules and horses.
This could only be one thing : a surprise attack with

the bayonet. A scurry of hoofs swept past me in the dark, scattering the ashes of the dead fire. And yet no shots had been fired. At any rate we should soon know the worst. If they had broken through our pickets in the dark, God help us ! And then a breathless sergeant ran up to headquarters to tell us that a lion had stolen within the perimeter and stampeded the mules. Their keeper had awakened to see the beast's great shape moving like a shadow towards him, and had cried out ; and after that the whole camp had been thrown into an uproar. If this alarm had taken a less seasoned regiment, a great deal of damage might have been done ; and as it was, I wondered what would have happened if we had been attacked that night, as ours was the only section of the perimeter on which pickets were posted.

Now it was impossible to sleep, if only for the cold, and at dawn of a most beautiful morning we set off again, following for several miles the uphill track down which we had stumbled the night before. It was strange how much easier the daylight made it—that, and above all the sweet and vigorous morning air. At the top of the hills we made a new line for the river, and reached, before midday, an open space, where for a little while we bivouacked.

Even so we were far ahead of our transport and our rations, which rolled up painfully, and by degrees. In all this campaign I was full of pity for the wretched bullocks who were forced to work (and there was no way out of it) under the most distressing conditions, growing leaner and leaner on the thin pasturage of the bush, and driven—for they were willing beasts—until they dropped. Here it was obvious that we had utterly outmarched them. For the greater part of the night they had been pushed and pulled through the sand of dry nullahs, working beyond their strength in a country that was waterless. All the transport officers complained that they could do no more, unless the beasts were to be sacrificed for the sake of one day's march. Indeed, they had scarcely strength to struggle down to the Pangani, unladen, for watering.

But early in the afternoon we were ordered to inspan. In this war and with this General nothing was impossible. Very slowly and with infinite pain we rejoined the old trade route, passing through a wide stretch of relatively open country, which had lain hidden from us between the thick bush and the Pangani. The track was level, and fairly easy-going, else our oxen would never have finished it.

At last in that golden humid evening, when the low sun cast long shadows, we halted, wondering what would be done with us.

Certainly something unusual was toward. In the clear sky an aeroplane shone like a yellow dragon-fly. The field artillery with their quickfirers rolled past, and, swishing through the long grass as though it were their natural element, a score of motor-cars loaded with the general staff, came by : the last of them, a grey Vauxhall, with shining pointed radiator, in which Jan Smuts was sitting, with Collier, his Chief of Staff.

The General's car turned through a lane in our ranks and made off towards the line of bush to east-wards. In a little while it was whispered that there had been good reason for our haste : that the Northern Army (as the Germans called it) under Kraut, was still in Same, and that Hannyngton, with the Second Brigade, was at their heels. Here was the defensive position on which we had expected them to retire.

Over miles of bush we could see the blue masses of the Pare, and in front of them, paler by contrast, the hill of Kitamuli, which overhangs the railway. There, too, was the great cleft in the mountains which is called the N'gulu gap, through which, by

now, the column from M'buyuni might be fighting
its way to press the German flank. And the
Germans were still in Same. . . . We were glad of
that, for it seemed after all as if we had not been
spending our strength in vain. There was a chance
of battle-fighting, even the chance of a debacle, and
our troops had many ancient scores to settle.

So we halted, waiting in the narrow grass plain,
and around us in the evening light all the mountains of East Africa stood waiting; and greatest of
all, Kilimanjaro, which we had almost forgotten,
rose like a gigantic ghost, sixty miles away to the
northward, utterly dominating, as we had never
suspected, all the country which we had traversed.
It was almost as though the great mountain smiled :
' Look what you have been fighting for.'

At this point it was decided that we should stay.
As usual a perimeter camp was formed, and soon
we were hard at work digging trenches before the
dark should overtake us. There followed a strange
night spent under the menace of surprise ; but all
of us slept soundly. Heaven knows we had earned
our sleep !

Next morning we had expected another early
start, for if our cattle were to be killed they might
just as well be killed outright ; but it was noon

before we moved off, and for this I had reason to be thankful, for the strenuous days had brought out a lot of old malaria in the regiment, while the nights by the Pangani had infected many more. We knew well enough that we should have to pay for these. A man may carry a mosquito-net in his haversack, but he cannot wear it when he needs it most, on picket duty at night. So great was the number of new cases that morning that I took special stock of our quinine, to see if I could deal with the regiment in what I took to be the proper way, giving every man in it a regular prophylactic dose. I found that if this were done I should soon be tapping my reserves. The risk of being stranded without any was too grave to be taken. So far we had been unable to evacuate our sick. The most that the field ambulances could do was to give them a lift in the mule-wagons, and these were already crowded. We were fighting time and superior communications, and in a struggle of this kind the sick men must fend for themselves.

And then, early that morning, Hannyngton's heliograph flashed the news from Same that the enemy were gone. Once more he had declined the pitched battle that Hannyngton offered him, as well he might with us hanging upon his flank. And

F

once more he had been too quick for us to threaten his retreat.   Forthwith the race began again.

We moved off, literally, rather lamely.   The regiment had been supplied with new boots only a few days before the sudden concentration, and to this extent we suffered from the General's surprise. Again the endless, straining trek began, through parched plains, through thorny bush, marching without recess from dawn to sunset for the space of three days.   And there is little to remember in all that time except dust and heat, the dreary bush in which the hornbills called to one another, the waterless nullahs running down to the Pangani, in which our transport struggled with sand to the axles, and the great motor lorries which followed us were left stranded like broken toys.

It was a sad land through which we passed, with never a single village, and yet a sudden wild beauty would sometimes smile at one out of its barrenness. In the bush there were nearly always butterflies, seeking aromatic honey from the flowers whose unchanging scent had become part of the desolate atmosphere.   These butterflies were very different from the lazy floaters of the forest : none of them were greater than our own Vanessae, and nearly all their patterns were variations of wings

By those sandy nullahs . . . clustered a green growth of acacia thorn (*p.* 73)

that were both familiar and dear. The little orange-tip, most delicately gay of all spring's butterflies, was mimicked here a dozen times, not only in orange itself but in bright vermilion hues, and in the colour of flame. Often I was tempted to leave our trodden way and watch these lovely creatures, for they seemed to be scarcely shy of my shadow, and ready to spread their wings beneath it. Quick and restless in flight they were, as are all the butterflies of dry places, even the little heaths and coppers at home. There, with the same slow, drowsy summer flight, a meadow-brown drifted by ; and I smiled, for I had seen his dusty bloom in many diverse places : in England, in Algeria, and in the southern island of Japan.

Other sudden revelations of beauty were there in our hot caravan. By those sandy nullahs where water flowed no longer clustered a green growth of acacia thorn, a tree of the most slender grace ; but here the moist air of the river or of these winter runnels had stripped the bark from their trunks, and left them mottled yellow. The effect of this was very beautiful, for it set in relief the natural grace of their conformation and gave to the whole tree, motionless in the calm of evening, an aspect delicate and ghostly. Ghostly, and a little sinister. It is

only in miasmatous places that the acacia sheds
her bark, and to the old hunters such as M——
who have tramped Africa for half their lives, the
yellow acacias are known as ' fever trees.' All
those reaches of the Pangani were bordered by these
sinister beauties.   Their trunks showed us as grave
a warning as the yellow flag on a plague-stricken
ship ; but we had no time to think of such things.

During all that march we were lightly in touch
with the enemy's patrols, and from time to time
small batches of prisoners were brought in :   a
sleepy German and three askaris, a group of ragged
machine-gun porters.   I remember well one tired
evening when we had marched into a patch of
thinner bush, where the ground bristled with fallen
mimosa thorns.   We lay in a little hollow which
had once been a swamp.   The black earth was still
marked with the gigantic tramplings of a rhino.   A
string of these wretches was brought in by the
Mounted Infantry.   We could see that they were
hard driven, and terribly thin.   Our men, lying
nearly as exhausted, were looking at them lazily,
and singled out the last of the pitiable file for
comment.

Our men were never too tired to make a joke ;
and the sight of these infrequent captives served

to remind us that the enemy, in spite of Kraut's most skilful retreat, was not wholly out of reach.

At 2 A.M. that morning we left our thorny bivouac and moved into a wide grass plain, where the going was easier; but by dawn we had penetrated the bush again, and the air was dead, and robbed of its freshness by the aroma of trampled brushwood. Then the melancholy hornbills began to call, with their strange drooping note, as though they, too, were fainting with the heat. We knew that we were in for a long march, for in this part of its course the Pangani is girt with impenetrable swamps in which we could not water our animals. On the southern horizon, right in our path, rose a mass of blue hills, a fine defensive position from which the enemy might well dispute our access to the water. Therefore we pushed forward with all speed in the earlier part of the day.

I talked with M—— of his strangely adventurous life. Thirty-five years ago, he told me, he had left the island of Skye for South Africa, and in all those years he had never been nearer home than Cape-town. Sometimes he had wandered so far south with the idea of taking the boat, but his plans had never come to anything. Elephant hunting, pros-pecting, sometimes moderately wealthy, sometimes miserably poor, he had trodden all the trade routes of Africa, and much of Africa that had never been touched by trade. He told me how he had lost his left arm in the charge of a wounded elephant, how his bearers had run away and left him with the poor pulp dangling, and how he had wandered for six weeks before he came within reach of treatment by a doctor who lay sodden with morphia in the wilds. Riding through this parched plain, spare, straight in the saddle, and easy for all his empty sleeve, he seemed wholly proper to his surroundings. Indeed, having lost his wife, he had taken this barren continent for his love ; so that whenever he had a little money in his pocket he must be trekking to some unexplored waste, not in search of ivory or gold, but of strangeness and unbroken solitude. He spoke a little wistfully of Skye and of her cloudy state, but distantly . . . distantly, as though her mountains were really part of a dream, less real than his own stony mistress.

Through this man of steel there ran a most delicate vein of romance, an almost virginal delight in simple beauties. He told me how, in his early days, before East Africa had been exploited by the makers of colonies, he had crossed a range of hills and dropped down gently, in the cool of the evening, toward the Victoria Nyanza, and how he had been courteously received by the Kavirondo, a tribe who in those days had not been abashed into any clothing whatever. He said that the simplicity of those people had given him one of the greatest pleasures in his life. 'A beautiful people,' he called them. Now in these days we do not think of the Kavirondo as beautiful.

But he did not tell me, though I think it my duty to write it down, the story of his latest exploit in the earlier days of this campaign. He had been sick and granted a little leave, but hearing that our outposts had been pushed into a new patch of country to the north of Kilimanjaro, he was all afire to see, and must needs spend his leave there on safari. One day a patrol of the King's African Rifles were ambushed by the enemy. They lost their officer and retreated. M—— was in the neighbourhood. In a few hours he pulled together the remnants of the patrol and scattered the enemy. For this holiday they gave him a Military Cross.

A grave man, with lean, serious face, and eyes of a very charming blue. The confidence bred of solitude had made him a thought sententious, and he could deliver himself seriously of all the old

heroic platitudes about duty, and the rest of it, of
which an Englishman is shy. And when I was ill
he tended me with a rare gentleness which afterwards it was my privilege partly to repay. He was
not popular in the regiment, for his native obstinacy
did not fit him for military discipline, and this
quality was the only one which many people saw
in him. They didn't guess, or at any rate value,
the fine flame which burned within him, the passion
which had made him suffer hardship and poverty
for the sake of strange beauty, for adventure, and
'the bright eyes of danger.' Once, long ago, he
had learned the Shorter Catechism.

All morning we talked of strange things which
we had seen in different corners of the earth, till
suddenly we heard, a little in front of us, a noise
like that which a careless boy might make, beating
with a stick upon an empty wooden box. We knew
it at once for rifle fire. The advance-guard were in
action.

Immediately the column was alive with hurried
rumours. A big thing. The Lancs had bumped
the enemy in a prepared position. We should have
to fight for the water. Twenty prisoners had been
taken already. After all, they hadn't been able to
keep pace with us. And to reinforce these rumours

we could see rolling along the bases of those blue hills tall columns of whirling dust. No doubt the main body was falling back on the railway, fighting a rearguard action. The rifle fire grew faint—a running fight that was passing out of earshot. Had our cavalry got round them ?

The whirling pillars of dust were moving with an almost incredible swiftness. Perhaps they rose from the cavalry themselves. At any rate there must be something doing, for here, their exhaust pipes spitting like maxims, came Willoughby's armoured cars. Perhaps we were in for it after all. . . .

But the column did not halt, and in half an hour some of the Lancs themselves rode by who told us the truth of the matter, which was that there had been a small brush of patrols in which they had taken seven prisoners only. So we pushed on, the Germans, on the railway, keeping pace with us, and barely keeping pace.

Another day of forced marching lay before us, and I think that this was the hardest of all ; for the country which we traversed was sandy and waterless and the day intolerably hot. We marched between the mountain which is called Old Lassiti, and the river, over a strip of drifted sand. We marched thirsty and with parched lips. A slight breeze made the spear grass quiver, but it cooled us not at all. Towards the evening one of my pack mules suddenly pitched over. It lay with frothy mucus oozing from mouth and nostrils. Three miserable oxen collapsed under the yoke and kept us longer. I thought that all had died from exhaustion and lack of water, but the Brigade Transport Officer rode past and saw the mule where it lay. ' Horse-sickness,' he said. Such was the beginning of that pest.

At a nullah of red sand, deeper and more impassable than all the rest, we waited, breathing dust, for an hour or more. I wandered back to the edge of the swamp, and as I stood there, conjured, no doubt, by the soft rustle of the stirred grasses, there came to me a sudden vision of that reedy Ley at Slapton, down in Devon, and of poplars sighing by a bridge. It was as clear and as real to me as if I were verily standing there on a still evening in summer, after rain. For all its beauty it was terribly poignant. I didn't know then that next day I should be under fire; but, standing there, I wondered if I should ever see the reedy pools again. It was after dark when we reached our bivouac.

CHAPTER VII

At this point, to my great unhappiness, I handed over my charge of the regiment. The officer who had been with them since they left Rhodesia overtook us, bringing with him orders for me to return to Nairobi. But now we were not only many hundred miles from Nairobi, but many days' journey from railhead, and it seemed too great a pity that I should not see any of the fruits of our labours ; so, like a bad soldier, I evaded my orders, asking that I might be retained with the brigade. The same evening, awaiting confirmation of my request, I was attached to the Combined Field Ambulance, and given charge of the Indian section, which was called B 120.

The change from regimental life was very abrupt. Henceforward I had to do with a number of African stretcher-bearers, Indian ward-orderlies and *babu* sub-assistant surgeons, Cape-boy muleteers, and a Boer conductor of transport. Nor could anything have been more different from the European conception of a Field Ambulance either in its constitution or its duties, for in time of action it might represent anything from a regimental aid-post to a casualty clearing station, or even take on the functions of a stationary hospital. The African stretcher-bearers, fifty of them, were untrained, and ready to disappear into the bush on the approach of danger. Only one European medical officer was allotted to each section; the only technical assistance on which he could count was that of two half-educated *babus*. But I was glad, at any rate, that I should still keep company with the brigade, and help to receive the sick and wounded of the regiment.

On the morning of the twenty-ninth we set out at daybreak from the camp between Old Lassiti and the river. In the dark we had quite missed the loveliness of that place, but now, in a faint light, and with many birds singing, we could see the lower slopes of the mountain crossed by a band of horizontal cloud from which little fleeces spilled over, and all the hillside below blue-black and washed with milky vapour, as are the flanks of the Old Red Sandstone hills in Wales.

I walked in front of the whole caravan, behind me the stretcher-bearers in ragged fours, led by their *Neapara* or headman, carrying a furled Red Cross flag. That morning they were very happy, talking and laughing together; and wondering what they were all thinking about, I listened. and found that they

were all talking of places : of Kampala, of Nairobi,
and of the camps of M'buyuni and Taveta. But most
of all they spoke of distant places, and chiefly
Kisumu, the capital of their own Kavirondo country.
When all this wretched business is over, I thought,
there will be great tales in Kisumu. But what in-
trigued me even more was to realise that these
primitive people, who, only a few years ago, were
walking in nakedness, were not only afflicted with
the same nostalgia as myself, but found some relief
from its twinges in thinking of places which they had
loved and left, and in speaking of them too. For
places, both strange and familiar places, had always
meant more to me than anything else in life : the
mere seeing of some new country—an unfamiliar
village in a loved county, or even a new street in
an old city, being something of an adventure. These
stretcher-bearers, like myself, were out to see the
world : they, like me, would carry home memories
that they would treasure, a great hoard of sub-con-
scious wealth ; and, perhaps, some day, in a village by
the shores of the Nyanza, drowsy, and gorged with
m'hindi, one of them would dream of this cool morning under Old Lassiti, just as I had dreamed the
other night of Slapton Ley.

All through the Pangani trek I carried in my

haversack one book, a thin paper copy of the *Oxford Book of Verse*, but what I read more often, in the little light that was left for reading, was a small-scale Bartholomew map of England, finely coloured with mountains and meadowland and seas, and there I would travel magical roads, crossing the Pennines or lazing through the blossomy vale of Evesham, or facing the salt breeze on the flat top of Mendip at will. In these rapt moments the whole campaign would seem to me nothing but a sort of penance by means of which I might attain to those ' blue, remembered hills.'

All that morning we were marching into the neck of the bottle, bent eastward by the sweep of the Pangani. At first the going was hard, over level spaces of short grass with driven sand between; but from this we passed to a kind of open slade where tall grasses bent and rippled in the wind like a mowing meadow at home. The lower air was full of dragonflies. We could hear the brittle note of their stretched wings above the soft tremor of grasses swaying slowly as if they were in love with the laziness of their own soft motion. Clinging to the heads of these grasses, and swaying as they swayed, were many beetles—brilliant creatures with wing-cases blue-black and barred with the crimson of the cinnabar moth. As we marched through the lane which we had trampled in those meadows they clung to their swaying grasses and took no heed of us though we had trodden their brothers to death in thousands. It was a wonderful day for them : the one day, perhaps, for which they had been created ; and so, in a warm breeze blowing from the south, they swung their cinnabar bodies to the sun.

And from this, again, we passed to an upland, scattered with the bush, where the soil was like ochre, and an ochreous dust rose from our column and drifted away on the warm wind. It seemed as if we were too late again. There below us lay the valley through which the railway ran. There, with their rugged outlines shagged with forest, stood the South Pare Mountains. This was the point at which the enemy must make a serious stand, the point at which, if we had been moving fast enough— and heaven knows we couldn't have moved faster— we might even cut him off. But the column moved on without stopping into the narrow bottle neck ; which, surely, could never have happened if the enemy were there, and particularly since our heavier transport was following close behind, struggling now through the edge of the bush, and churning up the ochreous dust into the air.

We had never before been so near the Pare range. Very soft and summery it looked with its fair fantastic outlines against a blue sky. The whole of it was softened by dense patches of forest, except in one place where a slab of bare rock rose perpendicularly for several hundred feet. Watching these mountains, and enchanted by their beauty, I suddenly saw a little puff of smoke drifting away from the lower part of this sheer face.

' There 's somebody there, at any rate,' I said to H . . . with whom I was walking. He shook his head. ' A bit of cloud,' he said, ' or perhaps a native's fire.'

We heard a distant boom.

' We 're not too late after all. . . .'

' No . . . I suppose that 's the bridge at Mikocheni.'

He had scarcely finished speaking when a great explosion on our right cut him short. Not many yards away a column of dust and black smoke shot up into the air.

' Good Lord . . . the blighters are having a plug at us.'

They had not gone after all.

It seemed that we had actually caught up with them, that we had moved too fast for their railway, and that they must now put up a rearguard action or leave their equipment behind.

Another shell and yet another screamed over our heads. This time their direction was perfect, and very soon they picked up the range as well. Four-point-one shells, high explosive: the *Königsberg's* legacy. Most of them were bursting well behind us, and we knew that our dust-raising transport must be getting it; but it was evident that the observer whose puffs of smoke I had seen from the cliff-side, must have had a good view of all our column, for the bush was fairly open and all the later units had their share of shelling.

With these things sailing over us, or sometimes bursting very near our track, we pushed on into a thicker patch of bush. It was now early afternoon, and we were ordered to halt and take what shade or cover we could find.

All that afternoon the four-inch boomed away; and once, for a short time, we heard the sharper explosion of our own mountain guns. We realised well enough that neither they, nor for that matter any of our artillery, could touch their naval guns, which can fire effectively at twelve thousand yards range; but we knew that the mountain gunners must be firing at something and that encouraged us.

G

All our ambulance lay scattered through the bush. Only the bearer subdivision of my section stood ready with their stretchers. Nor had they long to wait, for in a little while there came a call for stretchers, and I went out with the bearers to collect wounded. This was the first time that such work had fallen to my lot. One felt rather adventurous and small, moving out of the bush into a wide open space on which the mountain observation post looked down. It seemed, somehow, as if one were actually less protected from the bursting shells in the open than under the trees : which was ridiculous, for none of those thin branches could stay a flying fragment. We moved on at a steady pace over the rough grass. We could not have been walking there, along the edge of the Pare, on a more peerless day. The cool breeze of the afternoon swept all the grasses ; the aromatic scent of the brushwood, thus diluted, suggested nothing more than bland summer weather.

At last we came to the first casualty, a sowar of the Indian Cavalry, but not, as it happened, one of their handsome, sinister Pathans. He was a Punjabi Musulman, one of that people which is the backbone of the Indian Army, and his name was Hasmali. Actually he had ridden past the face of

.

the enemy's position, within range of Tanda station, and the shot in the abdomen which had laid him out had been fired while he was aiming at the engine driver of the last train. He thought that he had hit him too. Wounded, he galloped back, sprawling, a dead weight, on the horse's neck, until he reached the place where we found him. Now his dark eyes, of a brown that was hardly human, were full of pain, and more than pain, anxiety—as though he couldn't quite feel sure what would be the end of it. But *I* could . . . I was suddenly very sorry for the sowar Hasmali, and particularly when I saw his horse, a chestnut, most beautifully groomed, standing by with all its barbarous caparisons. Far more terrible to me than death was the sight of that apprehension in those brown eyes.

We carried him back over the same open space, breathing of summer. His horse followed meekly behind with long strides. We should not have taken the horse with us, but the beast wanted to come. Under an acacia thorn we hid the stretcher and gave him morphia, plenty of it, and dressed him. At first he was distressed, even more than by the pain of his wound, because we must uncover him. His native modesty was stronger even than his anxiety : but we gently persuaded him and the pain was too strong, and he yielded to us. In his agony he cried ' Aiai, aiai,' like any martyr in Greek tragedy. I think I shall remember the eyes of Hasmali, sowar of the 17th Cavalry, as long as I live.

It was nearly sundown when the order came for us to advance. Sheppard's Brigade had taken up a position in the loop of the Pangani, and the rest of us were going to encamp on the slightly higher ground which the enemy were still shelling. Our long column unwound itself from the tangles in which it had lain all afternoon, and as our dust rose the German gunners found us again.

To approach the new bivouac our transport must climb a steep and dusty hillside ; and as we doubted if our cattle, already so fatigued, could drag the wagons through the dust, I stayed behind with half my bearers to put shoulders to the wheels. Every minute the sky was darkening. The four-inch shells were travelling overhead with a whisper which resembled that of silk tearing. I stood on the hillside waiting while the ammunition column stumbled past, the poor lank mules, the panting oxen. Apart from the gunfire that evening was extraordinarily quiet.

At the spot where I was waiting, a little thorn-tree stood up against the orange sky, a straggling bush of many branches, from the ends of which the plaited nests of the bottle-bird hung like so many flagons of Chianti. In passing, one of our men had carelessly torn the bottom from one of them and all the flight of weavers had left the tree. But now, seeing that our column was endless, the owners of that broken home had returned, and were fluttering, from below, about the place where once their door had been. It seemed as if they couldn't believe the ruthless hurt that had been done them. I watched the sweet, bewildered fluttering of these small birds against the orange sunset. A native boy came up the path singing to himself. When he saw the unhappy weaver-birds he stopped his singing. He stood utterly still, his face uplifted under the branches, watching them. Then, very gently he put up his arm beneath the tired flutterers. I could see the whole picture, the native's thick lips parted in expectancy, and the wings of the homeless weaver-birds, in silhouette. Then one of the little things, tired with so much futile fluttering, dropped down gently to the perch of the boy's finger and rested there. This was the moment for which the bushman's instinct had been waiting. Very softly he lowered his arm, until the bird was within reach of the other hand : but, as he made a swift movement to grasp it, it darted away. . . . In a second the delicate silhouette was broken.

There I waited until the last of our bullock carts had swayed past. By this time it was quite dark, and I hurried on to see where the rest of our column had got to. The stretcher-bearers of all three sections were nowhere to be seen : but the ambulance wagons, with their teams of eight mules, still plodded along in the rear of the ammunition carts. The enemy had now ceased firing : the trick of midnight bombardments by the map was one which they learned later. There seemed to be a definite track which the people in front of us were using, and so we marched on for a long way in the dark. As we went forward this track grew more narrow, the road more difficult to clear. But in the end we came to a deep nullah, at which the first of our ambulances stopped. The wheel base of the wagon was so long as to make it impossible to clear the channel which was as narrow as a trench. The Cape-boys lashed at their mules with long thongs, and the poor beasts, who could not move forward, plunged into the thorn at the side of the track, breaking the hood of the ambulance under which our patients were lying. Plainly we couldn't go forward. Plainly, too, we could not turn a team of eight mules in a track less than ten feet wide. Meanwhile, I supposed we were holding up the rest of the divisional transport. Either we must hack a way through the thorn—no easy matter in that pitchy night—or else we must stay where we were till daybreak. We wondered that we should ever have been expected to bring wheeled transport along such a road.

Then came a staff officer, who wanted to know where the hell we were all going to. I had hoped that he would have been able to tell me.

' God knows how any one 's going to get out of this mess,' he said.

' Isn't this the way to the brigade's camp ? '

' No. . . . It 's the way to the water. You can't go anywhere except into the Pangani down there. And a devil of a steep hill.'

' I 'd better turn. . . .'

' Turn ? You can't turn. You 'd better stay here until you 're told to move. For God's sake don't go and make it worse.'

' Where is the camp then ? '

' Oh, somewhere . . . anywhere on this blasted hill. They 're all making little camps of their own.'

He rode off to find somebody else more worth cursing.

It was cheering in a way to know that we were
no worse off than most of the others. As for the
ammunition column which had led us into that
blind alley, they were even more deeply mired than
ourselves. And the real fun of the evening would
begin when the transport animals of the division
came down the blocked road to water.

I told the conductor to hold fast, deciding to beat
about the hill until I found our lost stretcher-
bearers. I had gathered that we were somewhere
to the right of the place in which they had landed,
and so I followed the old track backwards for a
mile or so, hoping to find some traces of the point
at which they had left it. But though this task
might have been easy in the daytime, in that dense
night it was nearly impossible. The track was so
narrow, and the surrounding bush so thick that
in many places I could not push my way on either
side of the carts which blocked the way, and had
perforce to climb over their tailboards and walk
along the pole between the sweating oxen. And
when I had travelled a mile or more backwards I
had still failed to find any branching of the road
down which our bearers might have wandered.
I therefore determined to trust to luck and a
rough idea of the map, and cut across country

in the direction where I supposed their camp
to be.

In those days I knew little about bush, else I
had realised how hopeless was my undertaking
In the darkness, even though the thorn was scattered
with wide grassy lacunae, walking was difficult,
and soon my knees were torn, for I could not see
the brushwood that grew knee high and hindered
my steps. I walked perhaps for an hour, but
under those circumstances one does not measure
time, and neither saw light nor heard the least
sound. I steered by the Southern Cross and by
the planet Jupiter which hung near by. At last,
with a suddenness which was curious, I heard
the creaking of wheels. Somewhere not very far
away transport was on the move, transport which
had avoided the blind alley in which we had stuck.
I was a long time finding it, but emerged, at last,
upon a track over which many wheels had passed.
I stooped in the darkness and felt the grasses to see
in which direction they had been swept at the sides,
and having settled this question, set off along the
track until I overtook a tired string of bullocks.
The drivers were Indians, and I could not find where
they were going from them, but at last I came upon
a corporal who assured me that this was the way to

the camp, though which camp he could not say. And so I followed them to a dip in the land over which other transport animals, in front of them, were struggling. At the top of the rise many fires were burning. This I was told was the Fusiliers' camp. Nobody except the Fusiliers was there, but a little further on I should find General Headquarters. Sheppard's Brigade, and, probably, the rest of my unit lay some four miles away to southward. They were sitting on one side of the Pangani, the enemy on the other, and both were hard at work sniping. Nobody in this part of the world seemed inclined to help me.

I turned back along the same road. It seemed that I could do nothing better than rejoin my tangled transport. A mile or so down that dark track I came upon another train of struggling A.T. carts. They halted for a little rest.

' Who are you ? ' I said.

' Rhodesians.' And very surly Rhodesians.

' Thank the Lord. . . . Is Mr. B. . . . there ? '

And a moment later I heard B. . . .'s homely Somerset voice with its reassuring ' burr.' ' Hullo, Doc ! ' it said. ' Is this anywhere near our camp ? '

I told him that we were near General Headquarters and the Fusiliers, and that Sheppard's Brigade was supposed to be nearer the river, four miles or more away.

' The main thing is, have you any food ? '

' No, this is the second line. Rations are with the first.'

They passed on, and in a little while I heard their creaking wheels no more. And then, strangely enough, taking a cross cut through the bush, I stumbled on H. . . ., the commander of our British section, who had been wandering round in search of me and the lost transport, and in the process had lost himself. With some difficulty we managed to steer back to the place where I had left the column halted, only to find that it had vanished. There was no doubt about the place. Here was the trampled road among the thorns, the ruts of the wheels were there, and even the terrible nullah in which the ambulance had been broken.

' Well now,' I said, ' have you any idea where you came from ? '

We hadn't, either of us ; but somehow we managed to roll up in the dark about midnight. By this time we had quite forgotten about food. We slept as best we could without covering. It was hellishly cold.

CHAPTER VIII

NEXT morning when we woke the sun was shining brilliantly, yet there was in the air that suggestion of a chilly mist which seemed to hang about the Pangani in all its course. We found that we had blundered in the darkness on to a barren shoulder of the hills from which denser bush tumbled to the river. After the coldness of that night, the sun's warmth seemed most precious ; and indeed its rays lit a most lovely scene : for all the ground on which we had bivouacked sparkled as though it had been sown with precious stones, being sprinkled with broken crystals of quartz. Some of them were clear as glass, others clouded with a milky white-ness, others veined with red or even redly tinged in all their substance. I stretched out my hand to pick one of them up, and it lighted on a fragment of pure silicon shining white, and another pebble of the garnet's dusky red. For miles and miles the high bush was floored with this mosaic.

For us there were no orders. Indeed it was doubtful at that hour if any one knew where we were, but we heard many rumours of the doings of others. We heard that Sheppard's Brigade had moved on at dawn : that all night they had been tried by snipers from beyond the river, that even now they were in action; while the Baluchis, and with them the Mountain Battery, had already moved up into the hills from which the smoke signals had puffed on the day before and were turning the right flank of the enemy position at Mikocheni. We could even hear distant rifle fire. But no orders came.

It was certain that we should soon be wanted, so we left our sick and wounded behind with an assistant surgeon, and pushed off in the direction of the river bend, where the fighting seemed to be. In daylight all that country which had seemed, the night before, a maddening tangle of thorn, looked extraordinarily simple : but we had slept, and breakfasted and the kindly morning sun was shining. Over the hillside we trailed until we struck a track of tall grasses swept smoothly in one direction, like the trailers of a south country winter-bourne, and we knew that we must be on the heels of the brigade.

There was yet another sign. As we approached them there rose from the thin bush on our right a sinister flight of birds of prey. They made no sound but soared upwards in widening circles, until they hung like kites in the shining air with their ragged wings against the sun. They were the greatest of the African eagles, the *lammergeiers*. But it was not on lambs that they had been feeding, nor a lamb that their eyes devoured as they floated far above. They were the first of many that we saw upon the edge of that forest.

In a little while we came to the place in which the Rhodesians had encamped for the night. We saw the deserted trenches of their perimeter, a few broken entrenching tools, empty bully-beef tins—all the familiar refuse of an old bivouac. And the regiment itself could not be very far away, for now we heard another sound like that of an errand boy trailing his stick along a line of wooden palings, sometimes running, sometimes walking, sometimes forgetting what he was about. Such is the effect of machine-gun fire at a distance. I thought I could distinguish the rattle of the German maxims, for in this climate it is difficult to keep the barrel cool, and they usually fire in separate groups of five. It was impossible to guess how far we were from the firing line, and so we halted for a little, in a shady place, at the edge of the old camp.

Obviously we couldn't stay there for long. The firing continued. There must be casualties, and therefore we must get into touch with the firing line. I took a little shaggy mule, whose name was Simba (Lion), and rode forward to see what could be done.

I had only ridden a little way when I met a big Sikh, who saluted and handed me a note. ' To all whom it may concern,' it read, ' The bearer will conduct you to the 29th Punjabis and 2nd Rhodesia Regiment.' I told him to lead on, and followed along a winding path in the forest with an unconscionable number of twists and turnings. ' These fellows,' I thought, ' have a wonderful memory for direction . . .' and then suddenly realised that we were making a line exactly parallel with a slender telephone cable in the bush. And now that I had seen this line which led, no doubt, from Divisional Headquarters to the brigade I had no further need of my guide, so I gave him back his note and sent him to waylay other inquirers.

The day was as beautiful as ever. Simba and I emerged into a patch of purple-headed grasses, moving with a silken summery sound, and alive with butterflies. On our right lay the Pangani screened with shadowy acacia. We dropped to a stony kloof, I heard voices, and stopped. The words were English. It was a little group of wounded Rhodesians resting in the shade, among them T . . .,

our machine-gun officer.   One of them with a slight
hand wound I sent back along the cable to the
ambulance.   The regiment, they told me, was only
a mile or so ahead.   A pretty hot time, they said,
in front. . . .

After the kloof the same drowsy grass country.
Suddenly—the two reports were almost merged in
one—a shell burst on my left.   Heaven knows what
they were firing at unless it were me.   A few
seconds later another.   It was all ridiculous, you
know, in that meadowland, on this summer day. . . .
At any rate the open space was so unhealthy that I
flogged Simba into a canter, and found myself over
a little rise, in the homely Rhodesian Headquarters.
The colonel gave me a smiling good-morning.   Very
urbane he was, and quite admirably turned out.   It
was the first time we had met under fire.   A tremendous crackle of maxim fire broke out . . . a dry
forest breaking into flame.   ' That 's the counter-
attack,' they said.

I pushed on, and found a little dressing-station
down by the Pangani.   They had hollowed a deep
shelter beneath the branches of a drooping tree, and
here, in the smell of blood and iodine, we were
busy.   In an hour the counter-attack had fizzled
out before the Rhodesian machine-guns.

The regiment had rushed the enemy line—had even reached the railway. We dressed their wounded under the tree's shadow. All the time, through crevices between the branches, we could see a fluent flicker of light dancing from the swift stream. A little behind the dressing-station a path had been cut in the river bank, and from this we brought cool water, in canvas *chhagals*, from which the wounded men eagerly drank, and we drank too, for the day had been long and parching. In the evening light I took back the Rhodesian wounded the length of the twisting telephone cable between three and four miles. To shelter the stretchers from the sun we had made the bearers cut the stems of spreading palm-leaves which grew down by the water, and over these we had stretched blankets. Ours was a slow return, but by dark we had them all under canvas.

And now arose more urgently than ever the question of evacuating these wounded men, and those sick with malaria or dysentery who were pouring into our tents each day. We had come down the Pangani far too fast for our communications. Rations were already diminished by half and likely to be scarcer. The railway had been so well destroyed that our trains ran no further than Kahe,

H

our starting point, and there the nearest casualty
clearing station lay.   The only way in which our
sick men could return was on empty supply lorries,
unsheltered from the sun, toiling with the utmost
weariness through vast sandy stretches and thick
bush, jolted without mercy in the deep nullahs,
sleeping under cold stars along the fever swamps of
the Pangani.   But it would have been worse if we
had left them to languish down by the river, for
already our tents were overflowing and at any
moment we might be moving on and they would
have been at the mercy of any prowling company
of askaris from the Pare.   And so, in the end, they
all performed that ghastly lorry journey of eighty
miles at an average pace of four miles an hour ;
and none died, that I know of, but the sowar Hasmali,
who might well have died in any case.   Such was
the purgatory with which our wounded men were
faced ;   and later on, when the line had been
lengthened again, their case was harder still.

Next morning we made a late start.   Many of
our tents had to be left behind, and staff enough
to look after them and, as a result of our lateness,
we found ourselves entangled with the two South
African regiments who had up to this point travelled
in the wake of the First Brigade.   We noticed, with

envy, the transport with which they were supplied. Their long mule wagons passed us in endless procession, filling the forest with dust.

Nobody could have recognised in the track along which we passed the tenuous path which, only a few hours before, had led me to the Rhodesian position. In a short time we reached the scene of yesterday's fighting. Here was our little dressing-station under the hollow bush with its curtains of broad-leaved palms. Here was the Rhodesian Headquarters, a patch of trampled earth. On every side were little landmarks which a few hours earlier had seemed of immense importance : the patch where the quick-firers' shells were bursting, the sheltered path along which the wounded had been carried, the ground over which the attacking regiment had advanced. All these places seemed to have lost their distinctive atmosphere, yesterday so poignantly expressive, and to have been rolled out flat (as it were)—so flat that they had no identity left—by the following army. Their individual character had vanished as swiftly and completely as that of remembered fields which bricks and mortar have effaced. I wondered how this could be : for it seemed to me that so passionate a thing as war must leave its ghostly influences even when battles are forgotten. But no man, in after years, will visit the battlefields of Pangani. No man, unless he wander there in search of game, will seek to look upon her sinister smile in the lovely winter weather of that deadly land. Why, even if he sought for traces of our fighting, the rains of another year will have hidden them in drifted sand . . . in drifted sand and in the springing green which utterly overspreads all these valleys when the rains are past.

A very peaceful scene . . . if it were not that beneath its peace lies hidden a warfare more cruel than ours, the perpetual deadly struggle waged between those lovely, wild things of which its beauty is compact.

A very peaceful scene . . . if it were not that beneath its peace lies hidden a warfare more cruel than ours (*p.* 106)

CHAPTER IX

By midday we had reached the railway, and there we halted for a little while by the side of a culvert which had been hastily destroyed—too hastily, for although the rails were writhen and twisted one could see that a little spade work would soon fill in the gap and make safe running, at any rate until the next rains. It was strange to look at this railway line of a metre gauge as unimportant to all appearances as any forgotten mineral line at home, and to realise that this was primarily the instrument against which we had been fighting : strange, and a little stirring too, for the fact that we were breakfasting by the side of that damaged culvert was a solid token of success. From the point at which we had halted right up to Moshi, under Kilimanjaro, this railway was now ours, and in a little time our trains would measure in a few hours all the toilsome miles which we had trekked down the Pangani. And after all, the cost had not been so very great : our casualties in killed and wounded were small, our sick no more than might be expected. While we could not deny that our men

and cattle were greatly exhausted, or neglect the
sinister suggestion of those poor brutes who had
rolled over and died with horse-sickness, any more
than our own consciousness that we had been forced
to sleep without protection in the shadow of the
pale fever trees, we had the happiness of success to
sustain us, and all the high spirits of a conquering
army.

On every side there was something to show for our
labours. Before the embankment of the railway
line stretched a wide semicircle of shallow rifle-pits,
littered with spent cartridge-cases.   In one of them
I found a box full of German ammunition, and not
only the regulation pointed nickel bullet, but a
number of four-fifty sporting cartridges with ugly
bullets of soft lead.   On the day before I had seen
the wounds inflicted, by these, and very horrible
they were ; but for all this I could not agree with
those who were shocked at their use in warfare,
for, in any case, their results are not nearly so barbarous as those inflicted by shrapnel or fragments of
shell.

Here, too, we saw the German machine-gun positions, most skilfully concealed ; the *bandas* in which
the officers had slept, the trampled circles in the bush
where their askaris had squatted, littered with husks

and mealie cobs. The sight of all these things was very comforting : and to give us greater cheer, while we were halted at the railway side, two regiments of the division swung by.

Two nights before, in the confused dusk after the first fight at Mikocheni, I had watched them marching in, haggard, footsore, unutterably weary. I doubt if there is any sight on earth more harassing than that of a tired army, its collective sense of a numbed pain that lightens into anguish whenever the auto-maton's step is broken or the worn brain forced to think. And now they were so different. It wasn't merely that they looked less wayworn or thin, but that a sudden jauntiness—that is the only word—had found its way into their bearing, making their steps freer and their burdens lighter. An extra-ordinary thing. . . . We had always been told that an army marched 'on its stomach,' but these men had been making forced marches and fighting on half rations or less. I knew then that an army marches on its spirit, and the spirit of this army was great. Next day, when they came streaming into the ambulances with their 'A touch of fever . . . I've had it on me a day or two,' we realised this. And if a contrast were needed, it was there ready to hand in the bearing of the wretched animals

—those gaunt skeletal mules, and wasted bullocks who followed them, and could do no more.

At a corner where the Pangani swirls in towards the railway, we found another surprise : a fine trestle bridge, unfinished, which the Germans had recently been building : why, it was difficult to imagine, unless they had thought it would open a shorter way to the Mombo trolley line, that very effective piece of war-engineering of which we had heard so much but knew so little.   Still, it was a beautiful bridge, the white planks shining in the sun, and above and below two reaches of smooth, swift water.   By the time that it reaches ' German Bridge,' the Pangani is a fine stream.

Everywhere as we moved through a dry, sparse bush scattered with raffia palms, we came across marks of a hurried retreat : the trampled shrubs, the worn road, the rifle-pits hurriedly made and screened with cut branches that were still green.   We crossed the railway again, at a point where a curve and a gradient came together ; and there, tumbled over the embankment lay an engine and a pair of trucks, terribly wrecked.   We liked to imagine that this had been the last train out of Tanda, that it had been in too much of a hurry altogether.   Later we learned that the exploit of its destruction had been claimed by the Flying Corps, and this, whether it were true or no, did something to heighten their prestige, which was lower than it need have been, seeing that their only targets in this bushy world were the tops of trees.

At last, when we had struggled through the sand of most frequent nullahs, we came to a corner, beautiful in the evening light, where the Pangani might be seen flashing between the upright leaves of plantains. Here, too, were the pointed roofs of native dwellings, and mealie-fields, waving high in the breath of the river. Perhaps it was a trick of the amber air, making all things mellow and lovely, or more likely because this was indeed the first evidence of human husbandry or tilled fields that we had seen since the long safari began, but the whole scene, in its evening peace, seemed somehow inexpressibly homely. When we came nearer we saw that the huts with the pointed roofs were empty, the plantains stripped of their fruits, the mealie fields trampled and pillaged ; and there, to recall us to dread realities, were an officer and two sepoys of the signalling company at work with a heliograph, turning that level sunlight to the usages of war. From the crest of a little hill that had slid down from the bulk of the Pare the Baluchis' helio flickered back. And then, to finish the matter,

a train of supply lorries, with no thought for the
safety of slower-moving units, filled the air with
clouds of dust, and a moment later we found that we
were being shelled again, luckily this time with a
faultier range : for a breeze wandering up the
Pangani blew the dust-clouds gently away, so that
when they reached the level at which the observers
on the mountain could see them they lay well behind
us, and shells passed happily overhead, with the
sound of a rocket ascending.

Darkness fell, and as usual the firing ceased. A
bird like a bittern boomed in the marshes. We
marched into a camp placed within a wide arc of
hills and bounded to the west by a reedy swamp.
This was the camp of Buiko, a mile or so from the
station of that name. All night long we heard the
naval guns bombarding the camp of Hannyngton's
Brigade, who had come down from the hill paths and
occupied M'komazi, four miles further on.

A singularly beautiful camp was this of Buiko ;
and there for a whole week we rested, beneath the
changing cloudy splendours of the South Pare. I
say ' rested,' but for us there was not much rest.
Now it was that the Brigade began to show the
bane of the river's sinister presence. In two days
all our tents were full, and we had packed off as

many men as could be carried on the empty supply lorries to Same, ninety miles away—a most horrible journey; and though we could ill spare him, we sent a medical officer back with them. In a fortnight, or little more, the Rhodesia Regiment had lost a quarter of its strength; the Baluchis, too, began to show the effects of their sudden excursion into the mountains' unfamiliar cold. We set our African stretcher-bearers to the building of *bandas*, which was an easy matter, seeing that we were surrounded by the woody bush, and the swamps, with their waving reeds, supplied us with thatching. And that, I think, is the thing which we shall always remember of Buiko, the odour of bruised reeds under a heavy sun.

We were told that it was difficulties of supply which kept us so long in Buiko; but I doubt if even such a thruster as Smuts could have got more out of the men who thankfully rested there, or the beasts, who now began to die in great numbers. At first we made a pyre on which they were consumed; but our sweepers were lazy with their fuel, and the heaps of charred flesh became, in the end, so noisome, that we had the carcasses dragged into the bush, a mile or more from the camp, to be dealt with by the hyenas and the vultures. All day long we could see little clouds of these obscene birds hanging in the sky. It seemed as though half the eagles of Africa had descended on us, and, in the dead of night, we heard the lions, who had stolen down from the hills.

A mile or so from the Brigade's encampment, near Buiko Station, General Headquarters were placed. As usual the Germans had wrecked the station, blowing up the offices, the system of points, and the water tower, and had driven away with them the native inhabitants. But one old man they had left behind, a poor devil of an Indian trader, who inhabited a shed of galvanised iron, with a little square window in it that served for counter. Of his stock only three commodities were left: soap, cigarettes, and Sanatogen. The first two were eagerly bought—it was sheer luxury to buy any-thing—the soap, some blue mottled stuff that would not lather, at a rupee a bar : the cigarettes, of black tobacco made in Tanga, at four rupees a hundred. The Indian told us—I dare say he was lying—that the Germans had made free with the rest of his stock, but in any case he must have realised more than his losses within a few days.

Each day we wondered how long our blessed rest would last. We knew it could not be for long.

The Germans, we were told, were still at Mombo—a place which possessed a double importance, firstly as the station for Wilhelmstal, a pleasant hill town, the centre of many plantations and the summer seat of the Government, where most of their women still remained; and, secondly, as the end of the trolley line which they had built to Handeni, linking up the Tanga line with the military roads which ran down towards the Central Railway. This trolley line was the means by which the enemy hoped to evacuate their valuables from the Wilhelmstal district, and escape with their force and guns if they should be driven from the Usambara. The trolley line, then, must obviously be our next objective. We had no maps to show how it ran ; but it seemed certain that it must cross the Pangani at M'kalamo, under the shadow of the Mafi Hills. This was its only bridgehead, and therefore its most vulnerable point.

The problem before us was not easy. To begin with, we were on the wrong side of the Pangani. Below us, for many miles, the left bank was guarded by a series of swamps ; while below these a tangle of mountains separated it from the valley of its tributary the M'komazi, in which the railway runs. To advance down the railway without any other threat to the German forces would be deserving of disaster; to force our way through the mountains would be nearly as hard, for there, too, a line of prepared positions faced us. There remained open to us the passage of the Pangani, and a continuation of the old struggle through unknown country and pathless bush, to which, now, another obstacle was added; for all that part of the Pangani Valley was infested with tsetse-fly, and we might expect to lose our horses and mules, and, for that matter, the rest of our cattle. If we should succeed in isolating the German Northern Army, we could face these losses with content; but here, as before, the first demand was speed, and with speed, endurance.

Already our airmen reported great activity on the trolley line at M'kalamo. It looked as though the Germans had determined to abandon the Usambara after all. It was even encouraging to hear their big guns battering Hannyngton's camp on the night of the fifth, for it showed us that they were still in front of Mombo. We did not know then that the camp at which they were firing was empty, that Hannyngton had moved out at night-fall. Nor were we prepared for our own passage of the Pangani next day.

CHAPTER X

AT dawn on the 6th of June the whole force moved out of Buiko. We were almost sorry to leave this beautiful and pestilential spot, for our days of rest had been badly needed, and in a short time we had made ourselves very much at home. It seemed a pity to leave our trim *bandas* there untenanted, to say good-bye to the swaying reed-beds, to wake no more to the sound of weaver-birds chirruping in the thorn-tree against which our hut was built. No doubt it was well that we left all these things, for in a few days the plague of flies would have begun, and increased the dysentery with which, so far, we had not been seriously troubled.

At any rate the camp of the First Brigade was a good deal better than that of the divisional troops. It was no pleasant experience to pass their quarters in the early morning, when the dank air of the river suspended whatever odours there might be of mules unburied or refuse unconsumed. There must have been a great many dead animals about, for at times the stench was overpowering.

We breasted the little rise by Buiko Station, and

117

passed through the garden of a bungalow where a white horse lay swollen with its legs stiff in the air ; and then, through scanty bush we dropped towards the valley of the river. By this time we knew that we were going to cross the Pangani. Beneath a great baobab we halted. A crowd had gathered at the bridgehead, and it seemed likely that we should have to wait a long time for our turn.

Two bridges had been built. The upper of the two was a narrow foot-bridge carried on pontoons, its pathway strewn with rushes, and on either side screens of palm leaves so high that a mule or bullock could not see the water on its way over. A little below this, and depending for its stability on the same pontoons, ran a floating raft, which made a zigzag course, swinging over with the swift current on its beam. Over the foot-bridge trooped the infantry and their animals. The floating bridge carried the transport carts, which were run down to the beach and dragged up on the further side by their drivers . . . hard work, since many of them were overladen for want of the bullocks which had died. Fifty yards below these bridges the sappers were busy on a third, which would be strong enough to transport the guns, the heavy wagons and even the armoured cars.

The Kashmiris were talking lazily together in Gurkhali

The morning was dull and oppressive, the Pare veiled in cloud ; but a little later the sun struggled through, making a fine picture of that gathering by the river, shining on the halted files of the Kashmiris, the variously dappled cattle, picking out the red armlets of the water police, whose chief, the A.P.M., was condemned to swing backwards and forwards across the Pangani on that little raft for two whole days. And there the river raced under green shadows. Above her drooping acacias towered the misty Pare, for now she had turned her back for a space upon those mountains. The Kashmiris were talking lazily together in Gurkhali ; the *drabis* were driving their bullocks to the bridge, and all the while the river sang its own swift song. Somewhere in the bush a hornbill called. In the foreground of our picture stood the Brigadier's car, and in it sat General Sheppard himself, reading a play of Shakespeare and well content. Indeed he had every reason to be pleased, for half the fighting men of the Brigade were on the other side already.

While we were waiting thus, happy, and a little thrilled to be on the road again, an officer rode down from the signal station at Buiko with the first news of the Battle of Jutland. We had nothing but Reuter's version of the Admiralty's first report,

I

and when we had read it our minds were filled with
a torturing uncertainty which shadowed the whole
of that day. For it seemed to us that we had
suffered a heavy defeat in an utterly unexpected
quarter. We had always taken it for granted that
' the Navy was all right,' even though it was in
spite of their blockade, and because of the runners
who had brought cargoes of munitions into German
East, and put new life into the enemy, that we were
still fighting in those outlandish climes. We didn't
forget that much of their ammunition at Mikocheni
had borne the stamp of 1915. If harm were done
at home by those misleading words, a greater harm
by far came to the spirits of those who were fighting
far overseas, and waited many days for reassurance.
And yet, in a way, the news was stimulating. It
made us anxious to be done with this side-show, to
have it finished once and for all, so that we might
help to get to the root of the whole tragedy, at home
in Europe.

By nine o'clock we had crossed the river, and
were skirting the margin of a vast swamp. All the
sunny lower air swam with moisture : the ground
was oozy and black. And yet no water was to be
seen : only an infinite waste of brilliant reed-beds,
standing up in the air so motionless that they made

no whispering. When the sun began to beat through the moist air myriads of dragon-flies, which had lain all night with folded wings and slender bodies stretched along the reeds, launched themselves into the air with brittle wings aquiver. Never in my life had I seen so many, nor such a show of bright ephemeral beauty. They hung over our path more like aeroplanes in their hesitant flight than any hovering birds. Again I was riding the mule Simba, and as I rode I cut at one of them with my switch of hippo hide, cut at it and hit it. It lay broken in the path, and in a moment, as it seemed, the bright dyes faded. I was riding by myself, quite alone; and as I dismounted I felt sick with shame at this flicker of the smouldering *bête humaine*; and though I told myself that this creature was only one of so many that would flash in the sun and perish; that all life in these savage wildernesses laboured beneath cruelties perpetual and without number: of beasts that prey with tooth and claw, of tendrils that stifle, stealing the sap of life, or by minute insistence splitting the seasoned wood, I could not be reconciled to my own ruthless cruelty. For here, where all things were cruel, from the crocodiles of the Pangani to our own armed invasion, it should have been my privilege to love things for their beauty and rejoice in their joy of life, rather than become an accomplice in the universal ill. I cursed the instinct of the collector which, I suppose, far more than that of the hunter, was at the root of my crime ; and from this I turned back to the educative natural history of my schooldays, in which it was thought instructive to steal a bright butterfly from the live air to a bottle of cyanide, and to press a fragrant orchid between drab sheets of blotting-paper. And I thought, perhaps, when this war is over, and half the world has been sated with cruelty, we may learn how sweet a thing is life, and how beautiful mercy.

By midday the air of the swamp became intolerably hot. We moved into a more open plain, where raffia palms were growing, and a single grove of palm-trees which was marked on the map had been chosen as the furthest spot at which the division could concentrate. The heavier floating bridge was not yet ready, and the howitzers, the field artillery, and our own ambulance wagons had been sent back to the German bridge at Mikocheni, which was now in use. At ' Palms,' then, we halted, not, as one might imagine, in any shadowy oasis, but on the open plain, beneath a cruel sun.

Flag parties had marked out the area of the camp

and the Baluchis were already at work on their trenches, when a message came through from the Intelligence Department, saying that natives reported the enemy to be advancing in force down both banks of the Pangani. At once the Brigade was ordered to fall in, to leave all transport except the first line behind, and to push on to the support of the 29th Punjabis who formed our advance-guard. This day, for the first time, I was left behind with my own section and the heavier baggage of all the others, to wait with the second line transport of the brigade.

I watched the long columns cross the open plain and disappear into the encircling bush, leaving us alone between the palms and the river. As we offered rather an obvious bait to any wandering patrol of the enemy we thought it well to retire a mile or so to the rear, where a great acacia stood up on the edge of the bush. Here, with a squadron of the 17th Cavalry for bodyguard, we settled for the night, feeling very much out of it, and wondering what was happening ahead. But although we listened eagerly for gunfire and held ourselves in readiness to advance at any moment, the evening was silent and unusually peaceful, with a pool of milky mist spilling over the tops of the Pare as

the hot cliffs cooled, and eastward shafts of the
low sun beating through copper clouds and washing
vast stretches of the dry grass in amber light.

When we placed our camp under the big acacia
we had not guessed that any village was near ; but
as soon as they saw that we were few, and not formidable, a group of villagers came out to speak
with us. None of them were armed, except one
small boy who carried a bow and cunningly fashioned
arrows. With them were several women, so laden
with watch-spring patterns of copper wire as to be
unapproachable but coquettish withal. The old
man was loud in complaint. He said that some of
our troops, and from his description we recognised
the Kashmiris, had driven away two of his sheep
while they were grazing down by the swamp. We
told him that if he applied at our camp he would
be paid for the damage done. He shook his head,
saying that he was afraid to enter such a great
camp, and then, to show him that we were in earnest,
we offered to pay him there and then, and hand-
somely, for any fruit or vegetables that he might
bring us ; but he swore that there were none in his
village, that the Germans had stripped their mealie-
fields and plantain groves bare, and that as it was
his people were starving. Certainly the natives who

came with him were very thin, but I think they were more probably wasted by fever than by lack of food. With a certain melancholy civility, he bade us farewell, and when they had moved a little way from us, the others, who had kept silence through-out the interview, began to talk excitedly. They seemed to be upbraiding the old man for what he had said, though we could not imagine why.

I suppose it was quite likely that the Kashmiris had indeed driven away his sheep. The problem of feeding a Hindu regiment on active service is not easy, for strenuous work calls for a meat diet, and to them the slaughter of oxen is an impious act—so that the temptation to loot sheep or goats for food was great. And yet, on the whole, I do not suppose any invading army in the history of war has behaved better in this particular than the Indian troops of the East African force.

Riding on next morning at dawn, in a green way, by the river, we met a strange safari of a dozen ragged porters carrying burdens on their heads. I wondered to whom they belonged. Half a mile further on the owner himself came riding towards us. He looked tired and hollow-eyed, but he sat his horse with a most beautiful ease, carrying a second rifle and a bulky haversack. We stopped to talk.

His manner was rather quick and excited, not in the least what you would have expected from a man who has no nerves. Yes . . . he had been behind the Germans again. He 'd been ' getting his own back ' (in a faint Dutch accent) for that narrow shave at the rapids, by Njumba-ya-Mawe. He had been riding seven or eight miles ahead of us, in just such an open slade as that in which we were talking, and there, suddenly, he had spotted a German scouting party : a white man and seven askaris. ' But they never saw me,' he said . . . ' Must have been blind. So I slipped into the bush and let them pass, let them get about a hundred yards ahead of me. Then I came out, came on to the edge of the track and followed them. The fools never once looked behind. I moved up nearer. Quite an easy shot . . . I killed the white man and the askaris ran. Then I rode up and picked up his rifle and haversack and the rest of his kit. Here 's the rifle . . . quite a good one. And here 's a vacuum flask out of his haversack full of hot coffee. Would you like some ? '

A nickel-plated flask with the word Thermofix embossed on it. And the coffee was excellent.

CHAPTER XI

THE spot which the brigade had reached the night before, where we now rejoined them, lay within earshot of a great stretch of rapids, in thin bush scattered with boulders. A pleasant camp, if it had not been for the intense heat which the moist air of the river seemed only to increase. Here we were well guarded, for the Baluchis and Punjabis had been thrown out some miles ahead. When we arrived the Gurkhas, of which the Kashmiri regiments are mostly composed, were busy catching the small blue barbel of the Pangani, and the whole camp wore an aspect of security and comfort. Reports from the front were hardly reassuring. The hills, which sloped to the right bank of the river in this part of its course, were stony and seared by many deep nullahs, which made it almost impossible to build roads for any but the lightest transport. For two days the 61st Pioneers had been hard at work cutting bush and banking the track, but they had not advanced more than four miles in this difficult country, while beyond the region of stony nullahs stretched a wilderness of swamps, impassable in the rainy season, and still, for all we knew, beset with difficulty. More than this we did not know. All the river valley above our objective, M'kalamo, appeared to be clogged with thorn of an unusual density, so thick, indeed, that aerial reconnaissance was useless.

But somehow a move must be made if we were to keep pace with Hannyngton, now marching down the railway towards Mombo, and slowly dislodging the enemy whom it was our duty to intercept at his bridgehead. On the evening of the 8th my section was ordered to move forward from the riverside camp (Kitumbatu) to join a flying column under Colonel Dyke, composed of his own regiment, the 130th Baluchis, the 29th Punjabis, the 61st Pioneers, and the 27th Mountain Battery. With us we were to carry rations for two days, but no other kit : our heavy panniers were to be left behind as well as all wheeled transport. We must look forward, we were told, to a march of over twenty miles through appalling country and a scrap at the end of it. Everything depended on the speed of our movement. . . .

That evening the light section, with T . . . and myself, marched on over the road which the Pioneers had already made as far as the Baluchis' camp,

where Colonel Dyke lay sweating under an awning
with a bundle of maps and airmen's sketches and
reports. It was a pity that neither were very
reliable. That night we made a cold meal of bully
beef and biscuit. It was the last food I was to
taste for forty hours.

We moved off at dawn, immediately in the rear
of the Mountain Battery. No Indian Regiment can
show a finer set of men. Sikhs, and picked Sikhs,
led by the best gunner officers in India and equipped
with all the care that goes to a crack corps. Now,
as before, our way was shown us by the Pangani,
beyond which, to our left, rose the mountain masses
which the enemy were supposed to have evacuated
the day before. In three places foot-bridges spanned
the river, at every bridgehead a village, and these
were so slender that we might look upon this flank
as secure.

As the sun rose the day became very oppressive,
with a clouded sky. Luckily, in this part, the going
was easy and the bush sparse.

The battery mules, with their guns in sections on
their backs, moved at a great rate. A tremendous
pace had been set by the long-legged Baluchis in
front, and in the first hour the whole column covered
more than four miles : a fine achievement when you

consider what one is apt to forget when thinking of all these operations : that the country was not only difficult but actually within a few miles of the Equator, at a latitude in which as a rule the white man rests under shelter from early morning till sunset.   Indeed the pace began to tell a little on some of our men, old campaigners though they were. In ordinary times we should have given them a lift on our ambulances, but here we had no wheeled transport, and the poor devils had to shift for themselves.

By eight o'clock we had travelled nine miles, reaching an open space in which the rest of the brigade were to camp for the night.   It lay opposite the mountain called Ngai and the village of Mheza, and we called it the Mheza plain, though it was really little more than an open sandy level.   When we passed by, a string of natives came out from the village over the foot-bridge, and walked alongside us with easy strides.   A very different type, these, from the painted Masai.   In figure they were spare and dignified, with the fine carriage of the Arab : their features too were nobly modelled as those of the Arabs, which showed us, if we were in need of encouragement, that we had reached a zone where the coastal influence was felt in physical types if

not in culture. All the men carried weapons:
spears with polished shafts of wood and wide blades
of an exceedingly graceful form. They walked
beside us, I say, and spoke no word; they did not
talk even amongst themselves, and, though they
bore us company until we were at the level of the
next village, did not seem to be very curious of our
numbers or equipment. Then they vanished as
mysteriously as they had come.

In the next hour we covered only three miles:
the pace had been too hot to last. And now the
character of the country began to change, as if
indeed we had left the highlands. The trees, even
the thorn bushes slung with nests of the bottle-
bird, grew bigger: their leaves were more green.
In addition to the everlasting acacia the baobab
reappeared, rising from among tall grasses. The
heat was suffocating. I watched T . . . riding ahead
of me on the mule Simba. He leaned forward in
the saddle as though he wanted to rest his head on
something. He didn't tell me that he was ill, but
I guessed from his languor and his flushed face
that he was starting an attack of fever—an old
enemy which he had reason to dread. . . . Thus we
marched, painfully, for another two hours, at the
end of which halts became more frequent. Evi-

dently the position was not quite obvious in front.
We were such a small column that the advance-
guard moved only a few hundred yards in front of
my bearers, and we were all prepared for action
at any moment.

At length we emerged into the swampy zone which
we had been expecting.   An immense reed-bed
separated us from the river, and beyond its belt of
acacias rose the mountain named Mafi, beautifully
wooded, and in particular a single peak with a white
scar of bare cliff on its face, of a peculiarly lovely
shape.   For a long time I gazed at this white-scarred
hill till I knew all its contours by heart.   And, as
it happened, it was well that I did so.   The track,
which was in places black and oozy as a road through
a peat bog, kept closely in touch with the edge of the
reed-bed.   It was narrow, so narrow that all our
column passed along it in single file ; and this part of
our progress, walking singly under the screen of the
tall reeds, struck me as vaguely charged with ex-
pectation.   Something must happen very soon,
otherwise we could not be moving so very silently
and so carefully hidden.   The sense of something impending was so strong that I took special
notice of the moment and of the scene.   No one
spoke ; the feet of our mules made no sound in the

soft earth ; but one heard the gentle swish of grasses
swept by the moving column. A pair of doves
fluttered away from the path. A flight of weaver-
birds swept the sky. We could hear the whir of
their wings. And then, without any warning, a
shell screamed overhead, bursting fifty yards on
our right. . . . This time we had not to deal with
the four-inch naval guns, but with the eighty milli-
metre quick-firer, which our men called the ' Pip-
squeak,' because the burst of the shell followed so
quickly on the first report, and its scream was so
shrill. Still we moved on secretly, and in absolute
silence. The Germans must have been firing at a
venture, for we were too well concealed for their
observers to have seen us. At any rate, now we
were in touch with them and matters might be
expected to move swiftly.

But the swamp ended, and in its place we came
upon dense bush, bush of a density such as we had
never seen before. To deal with it the Pioneers were
almost helpless. Even in single file we could not
make our way. And the enemy knew that we were
there. They must have guessed, for that matter, that
we were thus entangled. In that thorny trap they
might have raked us with their machine-guns, and in
a short time Dyke's flying column would have been

finished with. But nothing happened. Even the quick-firer ceased troubling us. The dense bush fell to absolute silence but for the lamentations of the hornbills, calling to one another in hollow tones. We moved forward in a series of strange gyrations. We stopped. To the torments of heat and thirst was added a sense of suffocation in the dead air of this close bush, too dense ever to have been swept by a clean wind, and charged with the aromatic odours of the bruised brushwood, a little like verbena but pungent, as the air of a greenhouse in summer with all its windows shut. We halted, waiting for a way to be found. Our Kavirondo bearers sprawled upon the ground in attitudes of fatigue. Poor T. . . . dismounted. He could hardly sit in the saddle for his fever was now at its height. He sat with his head in his hands. All of us, all of us were thirsting for air, clean air untainted by these vegetable odours and the stink of black flesh.

We moved on with a jerk . . . only for a few yards. It had not been worth getting up for that. And then we set off again for a hundred yards or so. I looked at my compass and found that we were heading due west, whereas the general direction of our march was south. We halted ; turned again . . .

this time south-east. Then due west again. We were wandering about in the bush as if we had been led by a hoodwinked man. In a little while, I thought, we shall find ourselves under their maxims. Probably we shall walk right into them. And then the fun will begin. Halting and struggling a few paces forward we spent another hour. Thank God there was no dust : so much, at any rate, we were spared. Several men were sent back to us who had been knocked out by the sun . . . sun and exhaustion, and want of food : it came to the same thing. And still there was no end, nor even the least infinitesimal thinning of the bush : just the eternal thorn of mimosa and acacia, set with brushwood and spearheads of wild sisal below, tangled with fleshy cactus above—scattered here and there with withered candelabra-trees lifting their dry arms above the thorn : over all the closeness of a heavy sky and the unutterable melancholy of the hornbill's hollow note.

But we had not very long to wait now. Somewhere in the thick bush in front of us maxim fire crackled out. The Baluchis had bumped them. We halted, unloaded the panniers. Obviously this was no place for a dressing-station ; but it was doubtful if anywhere in this unchanging

K

bush we should find a better. T. . . . was fit for nothing.

In front the firing increased in violence, its sounds magnified in an extraordinary degree by the echoing bush. Now our machine-guns, too, were in action. And then the wounded began to dribble in, Baluchis all of them; and our stretchers went out for the others who could not walk. Evidently, as usual, when our forces stumbled on a prepared position in the bush—and indeed the first evidence of its existence was generally a burst of maxim fire—they had lost heavily in the first minute. There was no way out of it; these were losses which were inherent in the type of warfare and not to be avoided by any refinements of caution.

Soon I was busy stripping off the field dressings and seeing for myself that the wounds were rightly classified. My *babu*, fat and a trifle deaf, stood near, and hindered rather than helped. The bush seemed hotter than ever. I threw off my tunic and belt, haversack and water-bottle and worked in my shirt sleeves. Two Baluchi subalterns were brought in on the point of death with shattering head wounds. A bloody business: strong and fair young bodies both of them. The aromatic air smelt now of iodine and blood.

Indeed it was hot work single handed ; for T. . . .
was as busy as his fever would let him be in getting
a shallow trench ready for the seriously wounded, a
pit scraped in the crumbling, fibrous ground just
deep enough to give them the moral support of a
sense of shelter. I worked may be for an hour,
may be for two. I have said already that we made
our dressing-station, as best we might, on the very
edge of the track which the Baluchis had trampled
in the bush ; and now as I worked I had a fugitive
vision of many men marching by, scarcely turning to
look at me with my bloody arms, the patient figures
of the wounded, the more patient shapes of the dead.
They swung by unceasingly and their swift, unending
progress carried with it a sense of gallantry and in-
exorable strength. I had not time to watch them
or speak with those of them I knew ; but very soon
I saw the striped brown flashes of the Rhodesian
helmets moving past. I could hardly believe it.
They must have marched like the devil ; for they had
started five miles behind us. Nor did they march
as tired men. The maxims were rattling in front,
and when one goes into battle one does not know
fatigue. And thus, while we dressed our wounded,
the whole brigade filed past. At any rate we were
well protected. But the firing never slackened.

CHAPTER XII

ANOTHER officer of the Baluchis was brought in with his thigh broken by a gunshot wound. He was in great pain, suffering, too, from shock of that surprise. The stretcher journey had shaken him, and he begged for morphia. He had already taken some; but I gave him another injection, for a wounded man will stand almost as much as you like to give him. About this time we found that we were short of water. That which had been jolted for twenty-four hours in our leaky *pakhals* had given out, so we sent four stretcher-bearers through the bush to the river with empty *chhagals* to be filled. In a little time they returned, very excited. There were askaris, German askaris, many of them, down by the river; on this side of the river, between us and the river. Several shots had been fired at them and they dared not go again.

It sounded like an excuse of the ingenuous kind which the African is fond of making; but all of them had the same tale, and all were genuinely scared. The thing sounded impossible. It implied a force working round the rear of the brigade of which they could not be aware. We sent a messenger straightway to the Brigade Headquarters. I do not know if he ever arrived there, but if he did it was too late.

Over the road on our left we heard scattered rifle fire. The wounded officer awoke from his morphia dose.

' My God,' he said, ' they 're coming . . . they 're coming.'

That is what bush fighting does for a man's nerves. . . . We assured him that it was nothing, that the whole brigade was between us and the enemy ; but he could not be calmed. ' Get me out of this for God's sake,' he cried. ' If they find me like this . . .'

We all knew very well what would happen if the Germans' savages found him like that; and so we shifted the poor beggar a little deeper into the bush, near the place where the two subalterns lay still with blankets over their faces. And he seemed a little happier, sighing with a sort of content. I don't know why.

Again the rifle fire broke out on the left : very near this time. Another stretcher was brought in, and on it a man with a chest wound. I knelt down beside him, and started stripping the bloody bandage

from his side.   His skin was very cold.   And then I
suddenly saw that he was dead.   I covered him with
a blanket.   The firing started again.   It seemed
very close now.   A twig, snapped by a singing
bullet, fell beside me on the dead man's blanket.
Surely there must be something wrong . . . and
then I saw some Kashmiris who were trudging
along the road drop down suddenly in the dust and
start firing into the bush.   So the stretcher-bearers'
story had been true, and now they were coming.
In a second the whole place was swept with maxim
fire, hellishly loud in the bush, and bullets were singing everywhere.   Luckily most of the fire was high.
T . . . was busy trying to get the wounded officer
deeper into the bush.   Another murderous burst of
fire.   We all kept low.   Indeed I was sheltering
behind the body of the dead sepoy on the stretcher.
The wounded men whom I had dressed and sent to
lie down under a tree were getting restless.   I
counted seven of them, all, providentially, with
wounds of the arms or body.   And then, without
any warning I saw the Gurkhas, who had lain firing
in the roadway, scramble to their feet and come
running towards me.   One clutched me by the
arm.   ' Jaldi karo . . . make haste, Sah'b,' he
cried.

There was nothing else for it   We must run

Our stretcher-bearers and ward-orderlies were scattering in every direction. I shouted to the wounded Baluchi jemadar to keep the wounded men together. He didn't know English, but for all that he seemed to understand. Keeping as low as we might, we crawled out of the bullet-swept area and ran into the bush. Five Africans who had been lying under the thorns joined us. We were fifteen men in all with one rifle between us.

We halted, breathless. For a moment the firing had stopped. Then they came with a rush, sweeping through the dressing-station, now inhabited only by the dead, and then, having found it empty, hot upon our track. There is very little about bush-craft which the German askaris do not know, and the track made by fifteen men is easy enough to follow. A pause . . . and then a few scattered rifle shots : the whistle of bullets very near. They had found us. We could hear them crashing through the bush. The machine-gun started again.

There was nothing else for it. We must run. At any rate the density of the bush assured us of relative protection and might serve to handicap the movements of the German machine-gun. Besides, I thought, they would not dare to advance much further behind our lines. In a moment their heart

would fail them and we should shake them off. We
set off, scrambling through the bush as fast as we
could go, and our pace was the pace of the slowest of
the wounded, a ghastly Baluchi with a bullet through
his chest. And then, to my horror, the bush suddenly ended. We came without warning to one of
those wondrously beautiful slades of waving grasses
with which the thorn is scattered. All down the
Pangani we had seen them waving their purple
heads in the sun ; but here the country was more
parched and the waves were silver. A lovely sight,
and very easy going ; but to cross it would have
meant certain death. We might indeed have
tracked forward towards the south and our own
firing lines, but we did not know on how wide a
front the Germans were advancing, and if we had
moved for any distance at right angles to their course
we should almost certainly have been killed or captured. Our only chance lay in keeping to the bush
around the slade of grasses. If they had any idea
of our strength the Germans would not hesitate to
cross the open ground and cut us off. But obviously
they hadn't. For one moment the jemadar, who was
the last of us, saw a white man with a maxim on
the edge of the bush ; then he disappeared and for
a moment there was silence, until the askaris picked

up the trail once more and began to search the bush with rifle fire.

My wounded men were lasting badly, and particularly the poor fellow with the wound in the chest. The bush was as dense as any I had seen in Africa, and almost entirely of thorn. There was only one way of penetrating it : to lower one's head, sheltered by the wide helmet, and dive through, heedless of torn clothes or flesh. As long as the eyes were safe, the rest of the body did not matter. But we were men unused to bushcraft or wounded, and whenever we paused for breath the askaris gained upon us and bullets droned through the wood, snapping the branches of the thorn-trees. It seemed as if we could never be free of them.

And I suppose they thought that here was a chance too good to be missed of taking prisoners, for they probably guessed we were a small picket party thoroughly scared. Our track in the bush would tell them, near enough, how many we were. If only that track could be concealed . . .

I ordered my party to scatter over a wider area, preserving as well as they might the main direction. For a little while they tried to obey me, but fear drove them together again ; scared men are happier in a herd. The main direction in which I had

tried to move was diagonally towards the north-
west, in which quarter our divisional troops must
soon be moving up ; but every time that we pointed
to the north, the enemy seemed to turn us west
again with their fire. We were like birds being
beaten from a cover. By now we knew that we
were quite cut off from our own people, and approaching, perhaps, the line along which the Germans
had planned their retreat.

And yet, harried though we were, I do not think
that my mind was ever clearer in its view of the
emergency, or, for that matter, more sensitive to
the amazing beauty of the evening, the blue shadows
on the mountains, the silvern beauty of that waving
deadly grass. I desired passionately to live, though
I hardly hoped to do so. And this was a strange
discovery that came to me : that though a man
who is running for a train or in a race can be utterly
exhausted, a man who is running for his life cannot.
So splendidly omnipotent was the will to live that
the flagging muscles knew no fatigue. It was now
twenty-four hours since we had tasted food, and
yet I was not hungry. I had a feeling that the
spirit of man is never so magnificently the master
of his body as when he is facing death. And still we
struggled on. The silver grasses became amber in

the mellower evening light. That was our hope, our greatest hope of escape, the falling of darkness. Never was darkness so long in coming. I remembered a poem of the lover Meleager in which he prays for night. And I thought of my wife and of our home in Devon, a drowsy afternoon of summer in a garden ravished with the spicy odour of pinks. A strange business this . . . a strange business, that I, torn and bleeding, should be running for my life through the heart of Africa, through dense thorn which had never yet been shadowed by man's figure or penetrated by his violence since the beginning of the world : while, at home, perhaps, she whom I loved most dearly was sitting in that summer garden among so many peaceful scents and knowing nothing . . . knowing nothing. It seemed incredible that this could be at all. The sense of the natural limitations of a man's sensibility, the mere fact that for one of us, who were so near, to have realised the other's desperate case would have been labelled supernatural, overwhelmed me. One is told that the instinct of self-preservation drowns every other faculty in a desperate man. It doesn't. Each moment I expected to be shot or taken prisoner ; but never, for one moment, did I lose grip on the imaginative significance of the scene, or of its beauty, or of the exaltation which told me that I might have been lying riddled with the many bullets which missed me in the dressing-station before the enemy rushed it.

And now, thanks be to God, the light was failing a little . . . for five minutes, perhaps, we had been unaware of our pursuers. We came, in the thick of the bush, upon a muddy creek, some tributary of the Pangani, with pools of slimy water clouded with mosquito larvæ scattered up and down. Down on their knees fell all my company, scooping up the water in their curved hands. I did not drink. I was thinking of the next move, and of how, if the fight had ceased, I might get them back to our own people. And I, who had always carried a water-bottle, didn't quite realise the preciousness of that shocking water in the dry bush. We heard a few shots on our left. . . . So we hadn't quite done with them. I remember so well the sight of our little group standing very still and expectant, listening . . . just listening.

We clambered up the far side of the gully and pierced its screen of thorns. Now it really didn't matter how much we were torn. But what *did* worry me was that the wounded men were obviously failing in their strength. I was sorry, in a way, that we had stopped for water, because that respite of a few seconds from the terror of pursuit had given them time to remember their wounds and to think how exhausted they ought to be. We beat through a few yards of thorn and emerged upon yet another little creek, or else a new gyration of the last one. And here I saw our greatest chance of salvation. We were, indeed, in a great swamp. I told the rest of them to follow me exactly, and led them a strangely twisted course, crossing and recrossing the gullies, turning sharp in my tracks, making an utterly baffling maze of footprints. At the end of it I felt considerably safer.

Then suddenly, we heard them near, and stood quite still. This, it seemed, was the end. At the best we must be taken prisoners. I nearly made up my mind to take the risk of going out into the open. There was one white man there, with the maxim. I might call out to him that we were a party of wounded and I a doctor; but my red cross brassard (if that were any good) had been left behind on my discarded coat, and I should probably be shot before I could prove my identity. One of my ward orderlies, indeed, was wearing a brassard. Supposing I borrowed this from him

before I stepped out. . . . Perhaps there were only
askaris there. A brassard would make no differ-
ence to them, and I should be killed, and the
wretched ward orderly robbed of whatever safety
the symbol might ever have given him. Or again ;
I might be saved and he might suffer. It wasn't
good enough. . . . Very well, let them find us !

They didn't. Dead still we stood, hearing them
come quite near. And then we heard them go away.
I suppose night had fallen. In the swamp, at any
rate, it was pitch dark ; and from the innumerable
slimy pools of the gullies arose a shrill chorus of
frogs. This sound, so characteristic of the tropic
night, made me realise suddenly the vast animation
of the bush through which we had been fighting our
way for our very lives, and its complete indifference
to the end of our struggle . . . so small a piece of
savagery in that cruel land. . . . It brought the
whole incident down to its proper proportion. It
would have been easy, I dare say, to indulge in
heroics or thank Providence on one's knees. It
didn't take me that way. I sat down on the
thorns—what did I care for thorns ?—with my
heart going like a steam-hammer, and laughed
out loud.

CHAPTER XIII

IT took us nearly an hour to disentangle ourselves from the swamp in which the enemy had lost us, for there—because, I suppose, the soil was better watered—the thorn-trees grew more densely than ever, so densely that it was impossible even to guess at one's bearings or the lie of the land. Far we could not go, for we were torn and very tired ; but in any case an African swamp is not the place to settle down in for the night. Painfully we struggled on in the dark, keeping as close together as possible, and pausing often to listen for the rustle of enemy askaris moving in the bush. Once, indeed, we heard a great breaking of twigs and a savage stamping such as no man could make. It was the noise of some great beast, a buffalo or rhinoceros, who had caught our scent and plunged away through the bush.

At length we came to a patch of more open ground, over which we moved with great caution. Here the grass grew high in slender blades that cut like a knife edge ; and here, concealed by its high growth, we found a dry nullah, with a sandy bed, in which, for a time, we halted. I knew well enough that the mosquitoes would worry us there : but we could not do without some sort of cover when enemy patrols were beating the country. Besides, we did not know, even now, what had happened at M'kalamo, or whether the party which had burst through our lines had been followed by any more considerable force which now lay somewhere between us and our friends. Somewhere from the north the rest of the division must be moving down the Pangani. On the whole it seemed wiser to try to join them rather than our own brigade in front.

But first of all my wounded must rest. It was now nearly seven. I determined to give them four hours in which to recover their strength. At eleven o'clock, in starlight, we would march north-east as best we could. Following this direction we must surely hit our own lines of communication. We lay down, all of us, on the sandy floor of the nullah, and then I started making a round of the wounded, re-adjusting the bandages which had been loosened in our pursuit. Four men I dressed, and then I became suddenly aware that two were missing—the jemadar and the man with the bullet in his chest . . . and yet another, an unwounded sepoy who had brought in the man who died on his stretcher, and had been caught up, as it were, in the stream of our flight. How they had missed us I could not imagine, for they had been with us—so much I knew —when we halted in the swamp. They must have lagged behind a little in the darkness and so have lost us. The case of the jemadar did not so much concern me, for his wound was slight, but the other fellow was a different matter altogether. I imagined him dying of exhaustion in the dark bush, or even lost and too weak to make himself heard by us. I left the others in the nullah and went out to look for him, very much afraid of getting lost myself. Keeping the bearing of the nullah most carefully in my mind, I made wide casts in the direction of the swamp from which we had come. It was all guess-work, for no one could pick up a track of that kind in the dark, and I dared not shout, for fear of the enemy. From the first the business seemed hopeless, but I kept it up for nearly an hour : the responsibility weighed so heavily upon me. It was nearly eight when I reached the nullah. Nearly all of my party were asleep ; the Indians propped up against the sides of the stream bed, the Africans sprawling on the floor. There was only just enough room to hold us all, and the stench of the Kavirondo was horrible. Nobody spoke. I had forbidden all talking : but sometimes one of the wounded men would

L

give a little groan in his sleep.   One of the Baluchis, a sturdy Punjabi Mussulman with a bright face, whose forearm had been shattered by a maxim bullet, made room for me beside him.   He seemed extraordinarily cheerful : probably he wasn't in much pain, for I had given them all morphine when they first came in, and I was thankful for that for another reason—I am sure they would never have stood the stern chase through the bush without it.

I settled down beside the sepoy, not to sleep, but to watch.   A most beautiful night sky stretched above me.   It was evident that my gully ran from east to west, for the Southern Cross shone very splendidly before me.   The night was very quiet (for I counted the high note of the frogs and cicalas as only part of its silence), the firing over by M'kalamo had ceased, nor did I hear any noises of the night's beasts except the howl of a hyena far away.   We lay quite alone, a rather pitiful little company in the midst of that savage land.   Watching the Southern Cross swing over the sky, I wondered at the strangeness of fate which had cast me upon this strange land, perhaps, . . . oh, very likely, to die there, and lie there till the hyenas had done with me.   And it struck me that though it doesn't much matter where or how one dies, I would rather close my eyes

in a country where the works of man bore witness of
his unconquerable courage ; where I might see on
every side tokens of the great anonymous dead in
whose footsteps I was following, and so take courage.
And this reflection brought to me a memory of old
Bruges, a week or two before the beginning of the
war and her most cruel ravishment : how on a wet
night two of us had stood in the darkness under the
dripping plane-trees of the Quai Vert, listening while
the ancient magic of the carillon in the belfry that
we could not see annihilated time.   We had been
talking of these things, my friend and I, and he
had lain gassed in the trenches before Ypres, while
I—but I was not out of the wood yet.   Both of
us, at any rate, had been able to put our theories to
the test.   I wondered if we should ever talk of them
again.   One thing seemed to me certain—that this
land was not one in which to live or die, being
wholly raw and inhospitable.   For that which makes
a place terrible or kindly is the life of men who have
worked and suffered and loved and died in it.   That
was the way, I thought, in which a country got a
soul : and this land had none.

At half-past ten the stars were bright and I was
ready to rouse the sleepers ; but I checked my restlessness and gave them their full time.   At eleven

exactly we were ready to start.   I looked up for the
Southern Cross. It was gone. Almost to the
minute the sky had clouded over.   I cursed the
moment in which I had taken off my coat, with a
compass in the pocket. For the present, at any
rate, I was in no doubt as to my bearing : for I well
remembered where the Southern Cross had vanished
from the sky, and often enough on dark nights in
our homely mountains I had carried a direction in
my mind for hours. It was worth trying.   And so
we set out again, stiff, and not much the better, I
imagine, for our rest.   At first it seemed fairly easy
to remember direction : but when we came into
thicker bush, and were led perforce through many
checks and turnings, I had to confess myself doubtful
of the way, though I dared not show any doubt to
the men.   Perhaps it was fortunate after all, for
the Africans were becoming restless.   They are
always afraid of the dark, and here the night was
full of more than vague terrors—of lions, which one
of them said he had heard, of German askaris, of our
own patrols. The last danger, I must confess, had
not occurred to me.   If we had approached our own
lines from enemy country in the dark we should have
stood a good chance of being shot before we made
ourselves known.   Frankly, I was beaten, and again

I remembered that in any case I should have to find the wounded men whom I had lost. The only thing left for us was to seek a place of concealment in which we might rest for the night. We might well have stayed in our nullah, but that was now past finding.

In the middle of an island of tall grasses stood a solitary acacia with weeping boughs. Beneath this tree we settled down for the night. And now that we had time to think I realised for the first time how hungry and thirsty I was. It was now midnight, and thirty hours since I had tasted food. In the morning we had marched without breakfast, since no fires must be lighted, and during the march to M'kalamo I had saved the water in my bottle, knowing that we might have to fight for more. Four or five of our party, indeed, had water-bottles, but only one of these was full. It belonged to an African stretcher-bearer, and its contents were very filthy. In that parched bush we were hardly likely to get more ; so I took it away from the owner, and kept it specially for the use of the wounded, who were already complaining of the thirst which morphia often gives a man. I gave them each a mouthful there and then. And as to food, we were in the same sad way. The Kavirondos, indeed, who are never happy unless they are eating, had a little rice in their pockets ; but none of the Indians had anything, except my friend the Punjabi Mussulman, who produced from his pocket three hot and flabby *chapattis*, the flat cakes which the Indians make with *atta*. Very proudly he displayed this hoard, and was for offering them all to me, as though I stood in greatest need of them. So that he should not be offended we divided them among all the sepoys, and I myself took a little piece as well. I had never before tasted *chapattis*. It was good to swallow anything that made my mouth less dry. Their flavour recalled to me the smell of numberless Indian encampments, the slightly rancid odour of browning *ghee* which fills the air in the neighbourhood of their kitchens. And after that I took a little drop of water. My God, but it was good !

The sepoy Kurban Hussein once more made room for me beside him. The night, he said, would be cold, and if I would do him the honour it would be well to lean on him. That would keep me from the ground. We settled down together, I with my head resting on his thigh, and so for a time we lay. He was a little restless, poor fellow, as well he might be, with his wound ; I expect, also, that I was a heavy weight upon his leg, for I could feel the muscles of his thigh contracting. I raised myself, and asked him if I were making him uncomfortable. He was indignant at the idea. ' You, Sahib,' he said, ' are a British officer. I am a sepoy. You command and I must obey.' It was the kind of thing which you will find in the conventional frontier novel, and at which people who have lived in India and imagine that they know the native mind are inclined to scoff. But it was very simply said, and splendidly in keeping with everything which this little Punjabi did. When he wanted me to take his *chapattis* and said that everything he possessed was mine, he meant it : and the man was not only wounded but almost exhausted.

A heavy dew settled and the night grew very cold. We lay close together, Kurban Hussein and I, trying to get as much warmth from each other as we could ; and a little later, feeling me shiver, he unwrapped his long turban from his head, and begged me to cover myself with it. It was only a thin *pagri* cloth, but enough to keep the dew from settling ; and luckily, it was long enough to cover the two of us. I used it, indeed, as a sort of mosquito-net, to protect my face, but without any great success, for the bush was alive with their wings. I do not think I slept at all. At any rate, I

tried to keep awake. In the middle of the night
one of the Africans jumped up in a great fright.
' Simba ' (lion), he whispered. I think he had been
dreaming, for I heard nothing more than the vague
stirrings of those untold multitudes of trees.

A little before dawn the birds began to sing. For
many weeks, now, I had been sleeping in the bush,
but never had I heard such a sweet chorus. There
was one bird which I had never heard before, with
almost the blackbird's rapture. In that strange
morning its song was of a peculiar poignancy.

At dawn I woke the others. Very haggard and
woebegone they looked with their torn clothes and
blood-stained bandages in that grey light. We
moved off through the damp grass.

And now another trouble began. I had determined overnight that before we made tracks for the
rear of our forces I must find the jemadar and the
other two men whom we had lost, and so I started
back in the direction from which we had come.
This didn't suit the Africans at all. There, they
said, were the Germans, and after a little grumbling
they tried to slink away from us. There was only
one thing to be done. I took the rifle from the
wounded Baluchi and told them that I would shoot
the man who did not follow me. Silently they obeyed.

At length we came to a track in the grass. Perhaps
it was our own, though it seemed to me too small for
such a number; perhaps it had been made by some
of the German askaris. Certainly it had been
trodden before the dew had fallen, for already the
spiders had spun their thin webs across it and caught
a little of the condensed moisture   Perhaps it was
the track of our missing men. But whoever had
made it, and this was encouraging, had wandered
in helpless, bewildering circles, as we indeed should
probably have done if we had tried to steer by our
sense of direction in the dark. We followed it for
a long way, until at last I saw caught on a mimosa
thorn a most pitiful piece of bloodstained bandage.
Evidently we were on the right track, and we moved
on much more happily. In several places we lost
the spoor. The poor devils, whoever they were,
had chosen a hard way in the dark. After all, the
bandage wasn't necessarily British; we might well
be tracking down a wounded German askari. But
soon our doubts were solved. Right in the middle
of the track the wanderer had shed a khaki frock,
to which was pinned the ticket which I had scribbled
in the dressing-station : ' Kaim Khan, 130 Baluchis,
Gunshot wound chest. Dangerous.'

This then was our man, grievously wounded, and

uncovered in the cold night.   I wished to God I had
been able to find him the night before, for now, no
doubt, we should go on till we found the place where
he had crawled into the bush to die.   We moved on
by degrees, the stretcher-bearers hacking a way with
their *pangas*.   At last we came to a place where the
grass had been pressed down by more than one man
lying, and here I picked up the calico cover in which
the first field dressing is sewn.   Near by we found
an absolute proof that three men had been there
that morning and were probably not far away.   I
was never more thankful in my life.   Nor were we
much longer in suspense, for soon after this we saw
the figure of a sepoy perched in an acacia-tree like
some gaunt crow, quite motionless, and watching the
bush below.   Hussein cried out with joy.   It was
the other unwounded sepoy.   We called to him
softly.   Yes . . . the jemadar sahib was there,
and Kaim Khan too, alive and well.

CHAPTER XIV

I suppose it must have been nearly eight o'clock by the time we left the place where we found the missing jemadar and the other two men. It was evident, by now, that Kaim Khan's wound was not so serious as we had imagined at first. Possibly the bullet had buried itself in the scapular muscles: at any rate, his lungs were not damaged. Of course we were by no means out of danger, being still a defenceless party in a hostile country, but our discovery of the others gave us immense reassurance.

The next thing that faced us was to find out where we were, and this was much less easy than one might have imagined, for the sun had risen in a white sky the light of which was so widely diffused that there was no telling whence it came. So we took counsel together and sent the unwounded sepoy up the tallest tree in all that part of the bush to spy out the land.

And fortunately there was one landmark which we knew for certain to overhang the road and the river, in the rear of which we must certainly find our own line of communications; namely, that white-scarred buttress of the Mafi from which we had been shelled the day before when we marched in single file along the edge of the swamp. At first it was so misty that he could see little, but when the air began to clear and the whole landscape grew out of the mist he had plenty to tell us. I sat on the ground at the foot of his tree, and Hussein, at my side, interpreted the words of the slender Pathan.

' He says, Sah'b,' said Hussein, ' that the hills are clearer and he can see now the big hill of the cannon. It is where he points.'

He was pointing straight ahead. Then that must be the west. ' He say, Sah'b, that near here (point-ing to the south) is a big camp. He think it German.' A long pause.

' He say, Sah'b, that where the firing line yester-day there is nothing. Over there (to the east) is a line of dust, a long line of smoke. That is the firing line to-day. It goes straight up in the air. There it is bad.'

' And is there no dust behind ? '

' He say, Sah'b, that there is behind a thin dust, going up two ways. That is the dust of ammunition column or transport gharis. He say that way is good.'

' Can't he see anything else ? '

' He say that is all, Sah'b ; and the dust which

goes two ways is far away.   But that way is good.'

' How far away ? '

' He say seven eight miles, Sah'b.'

Now at last we were in touch with something definite.   The Pathan slid down his tree, and we set off in the north-easterly direction, between the white-scarred hill and the transport dust.   The sooner we got there, it seemed to me, the better.   But now that relief was in sight our going became much less easy.   The day developed a terrific heat.   I began to know that I had taken no water, except a single mouthful, for thirty-six hours.   I kept on forgetting, to my shame, that the rest of us were in much the same case, that some had also the pain of their wounds to bear   but I was impatient to be done with the uncertainty of our position, and we marched, or rather wandered on, with few halts in spite of our tiredness.   Every half-hour or so we had to stop while the slim Pathan climbed up a new tree to tell us what he saw, and give us our bearings afresh.   To say that we did this in broad daylight may sound ridiculous, but there is nothing nearly so baffling in the sense of direction as this dense thorn bush.   In this same fight of M'kalamo, a company commander who left his men for a few minutes to rejoin the road never again succeeded in finding them.   In our case, too, the sheer physical difficulty of penetrating the thickets delayed us longer than our faulty sense of direction.   Luckily, two of my stretcher-bearers carried *pangas*, hacking tools of iron, and with these they made easier the patches where the bush grew thinnest.   To make a straight line would have been hopeless.

It was now eleven o'clock.   We had been on the move for six hours and seemed a very little nearer our object.   Somewhere to the south we heard heavy firing.   I think we should have heard it however faint it had been, for our ears by now were tuned to expect it and to take it for a warning to be ready to escape.   A funny thing . . . several of us thought we heard machine-guns firing inter-mittently to the north ; the noise turned out to be the knocking of an empty water-bottle against the Baluchi's rifle.

At last, about midday, our treed Pathan told us that about a mile away he could see big gharis moving.   The news heartened us all.   We set off at a far brisker pace, impatient with the Africans for the slowness of their clearing.   Indeed, often we didn't wait for them, and were torn afresh by the acacias. But what were a few tears more or less ?   And then,

suddenly, while we stopped, we heard the creaking
of a wagon's wheels, the crack of a whip-thong.
We began to run towards the road, as if we were all
of us sure that this must be the very last wagon of
all our transport and that to miss it would be the
end of our hopes. But sound in the bush is most
deceptive. Just as it magnifies the volume of maxim
fire with echoes a thousandfold, so also it makes
distant voices or other sounds seem near when they
are far away. Fast though we travelled, the noise
of creaking wheels came no nearer. It seemed just
as though the heavy gharis were travelling at the
same pace as ourselves and away from us. That
sudden release of our remaining energy had been
waste only, and we settled down again into our
steady pace.

Other things there were to cheer us : in a little
while we found that we had cut our way into
a new track running at right angles to our course,
and then another, the track of a single man walking through the bush—and not so very old, either,
for one of the trees from which he had lopped
a branch was bleeding red drops of sap, thin, like
blood. These, we decided, were the paths made
by our flankers the day before. The day before ?
. . . Oh, years, years ago. But soon after this we

saw, moving through the trees, not one ghari but many—the whole transport of the division, mule wagons, A.T. carts with oxen, staff cars, great motor lorries. A mile away in the bush one would not have guessed that any such mightiness was passing. And that alone will show you the uncertainties of the East African War.

By the side of this great stream we stood doubtful, wondering just exactly where we were : and all these people moved sublimely on, throwing us the tribute of a curious glance. I suppose we made rather a queer spectacle with our bloody bandages and our clothes in tatters. My knees and face were caked with blood ; so were my arms, and the back of my shirt was torn from top to bottom. This apparition accosted a South African transport officer, begging for water. He was a kindly soul, a little doubtful, maybe, as to my identity until I showed him my Baluchi wounded. Then he stopped a water-cart which was in his convoy and my men filled their bottles and their bellies. It was a great moment. Also he gave me some iniquitously hard biscuit made by Hardman of Sydney : a name which will be long remembered and, I doubt, has never been blessed before or since.

I gave the Baluchis a note and left them by the

This apparition accosted a South African transport officer,
begging for water (*p.* 166)

wayside to wait for the first ambulance backward
bound. As luck would have it the staff car of a
motor ambulance convoy now passed my way. I
begged a lift and obtained in addition a drink of
cold tea and more biscuit. We drove on very
slowly, until the officer in charge, imagining, I
suppose, that he was getting too near the front, or
impressed by my fearful example, threw me out
and decided to turn back. But I was not stranded
for long. Down the road—for by now our winding,
perilous track had become a broad highway—came
a procession of heavy traction engines, with the
Cornwall howitzers in tow.

I had never met the Cornwalls before. Indeed
they had never yet come up with our advanced
position, but I knew that a west-countryman had
some little claim on their hospitality, nor was I disappointed. Oates, their commanding officer, supplied me straightway with food and drink and
tobacco, and sent me forward to the front in his
car. I could not have asked a better fate that morning than to have met the officers of this battery.

When I reached the ambulance a message had
just been sent round to brigade asking for a search
party to recover me. I was thankful to find that
T—— had been luckier than myself. The German

M

rush had passed him by, and he was able to emerge
from the bush before midnight. Of course I was
quite prepared to have lost all my kit, my haversack, my belt and water-bottle and revolver; but
though they had been widely scattered I found
them all. My boy, to whom they had been entrusted,
had vanished utterly. One living man, a wounded
sepoy who had just been brought in on a stretcher,
had been left behind (we did not know he was
there) when the dressing-station was rushed. He
told us how the askaris had come swarming in and
how the white machine-gunner had lifted the
blanket which covered him to see if he were really
wounded, and had then passed on in a great hurry.
He had also lifted the blankets from the faces of
the dead.

Before I had finished painting my torn knees
with iodine, the order came to advance. With the
mule Simba I rode on, in my rags, at the head of
the ambulance, on through the bush where the
Baluchis had been swept by the German machine-
guns, past the German emplacements and trenches
to M'kalamo itself and the debated trolley line over
which, alas! the greater part of the enemy had
now escaped towards Handeni and the Central
Railway.

Little by little we began to understand why our movement, so nearly a success, had failed.

It appears that although we did not know it, there were two reasonable tracks which we might have followed more easily than our own hard way through the thorn : one of them, along which the Germans expected us, near to the river, and the other, three or four miles further west, cutting the trolley way between M'kalamo and Handeni.

No doubt our sudden emergence from the thick bush had been a surprise to the enemy, and indeed, if we had been better informed, would have allowed us to cut off the greater part of his forces who were occupying the position nearer the river. But the first people to know of this position were the stretcher-bearers whom we had sent down to the river for water. Then it was too late, and the Germans quickly turned our potential advantage into their own, by breaking through our line (as we have seen) in the rear of our firing positions and sweeping with maxim fire the road by which reinforcements and transports were arriving. And this is where the second cause of our failure is shown : for if the rest of the brigade and the divisional troops, following hot-foot on the heels of Dyke's flying column, had taken the westerly road, sweeping round in the rear of the M'kalamo position on our right flank, they might still have recovered the advantage which our ignorance had lost us. Instead of this they came rolling up behind, urging the spear-head against a point where the armour was strongest. And, to cut the matter short, at M'kalamo we made no capture except a single elderly German who was found sleeping in the bush. In the night all the rest of the enemy's forces who had just left Mombo in Hannyngton's hands, were hurried through along the trolley way, and not only their men but the big guns which had been brought over from the wrecked *Königsberg* to the Tanga line.

One thing, indeed, our rapid turning movement had effected. The railway was now clear as far south as Mombo, while Kraut's northern army had ceased to protect it ; but even this achievement was marred a little by our finding, from captured letters, that this move had been expected and provided for. Wilhelmstal, indeed, the summer seat of the colonial government, now passed into our hands, and with it a large number of the enemy's women and children whom he considered we could feed more easily than he. Their abandonment also implied an appreciation of our methods of warfare. I do not think we could have dared to do the same.

'We can see the lights of Wilhelmstal,' wrote Reuter, in a flamboyant dispatch ; and this statement may go along with the other picturesque visions of predatory big game, for Wilhelmstal lay many miles away and many thousand feet above us, hidden in the tangled Usambara, a township of scattered *shambas*, with no lights to speak of.

CHAPTER XV

WHEN we marched into M'kalamo the trolley station was still smouldering. The Germans had fired it before they left. A small bungalow near the line was also on fire ; it had been wrecked by one of the mountain battery shells. The *bandas* in which the enemy's askaris had been housed had also suffered from our airmen's bombs. This was almost the first chance they had had in the whole campaign of seeing a mark and aiming at it.

In a wide space between the line and the river the whole brigade encamped. It was a beautiful evening, and perhaps to me more beautiful because I had not expected to see it. Everybody seemed in very good spirits. The South Africans were shouting and laughing over the few trucks on the trolley sidings that the Germans had left behind, running them down a little incline and making mock collisions with them.

The trees by the river showed a green which seemed unusually soft and grateful after the ashen colours of the dry bush. Over the bridge, from the river-side plantations, our porters came carrying great bunches of bananas of a rich blue green, very lovely against their polished skins. Beneath these burdens they walked magnificently erect.

All these things I saw with the enchanted eye of a prisoner reprieved from sentence of death. I could look now with happy eyes even on that white-scarred hill which had overlooked the whole battle. I had a great and new zest for life, and all things that were puissant and living. I saw things and men with some faint reflection of the splendid atmosphere of childhood. I suppose it was too good to last. There came a reaction, and behold, I was nothing but a torn, tired man, a little bewildered and weak, and grateful to be alive.

That night I could not sleep. I was thankful when dawn came, at which hour we were ordered to set out again. It seemed that even if we had no hope of catching him, we must keep the enemy on the run ; but I was far too ill and stiff to attempt walking or riding. I travelled, to my humiliation, in one of my own ambulances, T—— in another. The way led along the trolley line, but going was not easy ; for the enemy had ripped up the rails as they retired, and thrown them across the road. Any barrier to impede us was valuable, and here lay one to hand.

After an hour or so we made a long halt.   Machine-gun fire broke out again, so we were not very far behind.   Indeed the 17th Cavalry had got in touch with them and lost an officer, killed, already. But it was only a half-hearted rearguard action that the Germans were fighting, and they did not delay us long.   By midday we had reached the point at which the trolley line leaves the Pangani, opposite the island village of Luchomo.   A famous camp this became in after days, for it was here that Brits and his cavalry sat down for three or four weeks, losing thirty or forty horses a day from fly.   A beautiful spot, but one as treacherous to man as to the luckless animals.   I pitched one of our tents there under a great tree not far from the river, and there I slept all night with the sound of running water colouring my dreams.

For the brigade there came no respite : next day, at dawn, they passed on their way again, but the ambulance was now so clogged with sick men that a section had to be left behind, and naturally enough T—— and I were chosen.   The fever which had begun with him on the day of the M'kalamo fight had developed into an ugly attack, but we had some hopes that he would get the better of it before we were ordered to move on.   I, too, was down

. . . through the greenery of the further bank . . . we could see the pointed roofs . . . of the native village (p. 175)

with dysentery. Certainly two or three days must pass before we could evacuate our sick.

Next day the divisional troops passed through, and we were left alone at Luchomo with a double company of Rhodesians, under Major Cashel, for guard. Three pleasant days we passed in rest under that spreading tree by the river-side. Here the Pangani, that swift stream, splits to enclose an island on which the village is built. Either branch is incredibly rapid, fringed with great grasses and overshadowed by forest trees. Day and night the sound of this rushing water was in our ears. A little above us the wooden bridge which the Germans had broken spanned the stream. It was mended now, and a sepoy, with fixed bayonet, stood guard over it; but through the greenery of the further bank, reaching into a soft blue sky, we could see the pointed roofs, like great beehives, of the native village. And at night we could hear the rumble of their African drums.

But even though these days were bland and sunny and the river and the mountains full of beauty, there could be no rest for us at Luchomo. Somewhere, a little in front of us, the brigade were pushing on through a country very nearly waterless, always in touch with the enemy falling

back upon his own lines of communication. With
the brigade I lived every day as did also the poor
Rhodesians who were left to guard us. All day
we wondered. . . . We need not have wondered,
for the experience of the brigade was only a repetition of what had passed before—thirst and fatigue
and endless marching under a hot sky, endless
wondering as to whether the transport animals
would hold out or collapse on the way. Two days
later, indeed, we were to follow in their steps, when
they had mopped up the little water that there was :
but we were to march without an enemy ahead and
on either flank. In a campaign of this kind, or
I suppose in any campaign, the only place that is
tolerable to a man is the front of the front.

For one thing, however, I must always remember
Luchomo, and that is the great beauty of the bird
song at sunset and just before dawn. All those
deep thickets by the Pangani were full of weaver-
birds and shrikes. The doleful cry of the hornbill
never made melancholy our days. One evening,
while I was sitting alone beneath my tree in the
dusk, a rain-bird sang near me, sang its simple
song of three descending notes in the diatonic scale,
thin, and very sweet, repeated many times. There
were lots of things in music of which this song might

have reminded me in its soft repetitions; but what
it brought to my mind most clearly was the sweet,
cracked bells of a village church, a little out of tune
(as was the rain-bird itself); not, indeed, of any village
that I know, but of a dream village which I am sure
I shall find some day, for I should know it anywhere. The church with the cracked bells has a
spire of no great beauty, and up to it there runs a
climbing street which crosses a wooden bridge at
the foot of the hill, where there runs a little stream
green with brooklime. And of course it is Sunday
there, for that is why the sweet cracked bells are
ringing over the mowing grass, and meadows where
the evening sun casts long shadows, and cuckoos are
calling, in level flight from elm to elm. Some day,
in a still evening of summer, I shall enter this dream
village, and my soul will remember how it had been
there before, while I sat dreaming one evening under
a great tree at Luchomo beside the rushing Pangani.
Some day, I say . . . but perhaps it will not be in
this life.

We sent T—— back, with much other unfortunate human wreckage, and the same morning at
dawn marched out beside the broken trolley line
towards Handeni. Ten hours we marched before
we came to the place where water was supposed to

be waiting for us. The country through which we passed was all of dry and fairly open thorn, with deepish ravines in which water should have flowed if one could judge by the presence of those smooth-trunked trees which grow in watery places. But no water lay hidden in these valley bottoms. We saw the dry black pits which those who had passed before us had digged there. It was not pleasant going. The heat was intense and the stink-ants so plentiful that all our way might have been strewn with rotting carrion. The Germans' road too was hard and dusty with the marching of the troops in front of us. Great gangs of pioneers and fatigues from other Indian regiments were at work on the road, for the Germans had had time to wreck all the bridges by which the trolley line crossed the ravines, and the rails had been so lightly laid that they had been able to rip them up again without any great trouble.

At length we came to the place at which we expected to camp and water our beasts. Beneath a flat thorn bush a major of the Lancs lay miserable with fever, issuing permits for the use of the water. The German maps marked here a permanent stream with the name of M'zungu-wazara, but all that the brigade had found had been a stony river-bed with

one or two rock pools in which the water left by the
rains had evaporated to the consistency of condensed milk. The brigade had taken first share.
What they had left behind was hardly worth the
jealous guard which the Lancs major under the thorn-
tree kept over it. When I reached it there was little
left in the rock pools but a sediment of black mud,
in which big crabs crawled sideways to and fro.
Obviously, although we had already done more than
a day's march, we must push on, or else our cattle
would have nothing on which to start next day.
At four o'clock, in the cool of the afternoon, we
moved off again. M'zungu-wazara was the only
watering-place for thirty miles.

We journeyed on and on, painfully, in the dark.
Two of my mules fell down and died in the road.
The conductor told me that others must die if we
did not find them water ; but there was no water
to be found for long enough yet. At length—it was
about ten o'clock at night—we came to another deep
ravine, and our hopes revived. To foster them we
heard distinctly a soft murmur, as of a flowing
stream. We were deceived, for the sound came
from a great plantation of mealies and a soft wind
moving through their dry stalks. My stretcher-
bearers scattered among them in search of cobs,

but found none.   The Germans never left any possible source of food supply behind them.   And yet,
for all this, the mealie-fields gave us cheer ; for we
knew that they implied cultivation and the nearness
of a village, which surely could not exist wholly
without water.   And there indeed we found water
of a sort, horrible stuff—but our cattle would have
died without it.

The place was called M'bagui, and in later days
became an important aerodrome.   We spent the
night uncomfortably upon a sloping hillside above
the mealie-fields.   As soon as we halted my ambulance was crowded with men whom the march had
knocked out, and for these I had neither water nor
food.   That day, and indeed for some days afterwards, our supply of rations failed us altogether.
For ourselves we had small reserves of bully beef
and biscuits, but the African followers had nothing ;
and the country, as I have said, was stripped to the
last leaf, as by a flight of locusts.

Next morning we moved out again over a high
rolling country from which many fine mountain
shapes were seen to the south.   It was a great help
to our depressed spirits to realise once more that
open country existed, that there was really anything else in the world but waterless bush.   The

character of the country, too, was changed. On distant hillsides we could see the pale green of mealie-fields, and the hillsides were all scattered with trees of a new kind. Here, indeed, the influence of the last rains had nearly vanished, for all these new trees were gently touched with gold or copper colouring, or sometimes the richer hues of the autumnal beech; so that we might almost have been riding through an orchard country at home in autumn, or, in other places, through a scattered parkland. And this high land was cut by sudden hills and valleys in which grew veritable forest trees. A poor country, I suppose, but anything in the world that was not dry bush spoke of paradise to our eyes. Over all these wide spaces the grasses stood still and silvery, very different from the purple-headed fields of the Pangani. Along far horizons we could see smoke curling where the enemy in their retreat had sought to burn up the land behind them.

But we did not stay for long on the crown of this country. Midday brought us to a sloping hillside, deep in dust. Four or five great lorries were stranded there and could move no further. Bullock-wagons were unloading them of the rations which they had failed to deliver. This sandy strip, than which there was nothing worse on the whole of the Pangani trek, made havoc of our supplies for several days.　Here too, over the brow of the hill, stood Willoughby's armoured cars within a great *boma* of thorn, their maxims pointing outwards.　On a steep hillside the whole brigade was encamped ; but my column had hardly arrived when they set off again, leaving me with more than ninety sick men to evacuate as best I could.　Now indeed it seemed that we were beginning to shed men.　Ninety sick men in a single day from a brigade of less than four thousand . . . this was the price we paid for our nights by the Pangani, for our lovely camp on the edge of the swamp at Buiko.　And so, once more, the brigade passed on, leaving us on the little hill named Kilimanjaro with one regiment, the 29th Punjabis, and our sick men.

CHAPTER XVI .

AND at Kilimanjaro, with the Punjabis, for three days and nights we lay. To dispose of the sick proved a difficult matter, for the general staff had decided abruptly that this was not the best way after all by which to approach Handeni, and indeed they would have had great trouble with the guns in the sand if they had taken it. As a consequence not only the convoys of supplies but the whole machinery for the evacuation of our sick was diverted to another road, many miles away over impassable valleys, and our small camp left stranded hopelessly ' in the blue.'

The problem of evacuation involved another—that of food. We had no rations for our sick men ; we could not move so many except on empty supply lorries, and obviously there was no hope of supply lorries coming our way in the numbers which we should need. There seemed to be only one way out of the difficulty. I sent back small batches of sick men in the mule wagons, eight to a wagon, as far as the place where the new road left the old   With them I sent a Babu sub-assistant surgeon ; and there, on the main line of our communications, they were dumped. At any rate they now had a chance of being fed and at last getting into touch with the motor ambulance convoy.

No sooner had we rid ourselves of our ninety patients and the problem of feeding them, than the Punjabis began to come in with fever. The last time I had sent in our mule wagons they had been retained by the divisional medical authorities, so that we were now without the transport to take our sick with us when the order to advance should come. We couldn't carry them with us, and yet how could we leave them behind ?

Altogether our isolated position on the hillside at Kilimanjaro was hardly enviable. Neither we nor the Punjabis knew exactly where the rest of our forces were ; and it seemed as if these also had forgotten our existence, for no supplies came to feed us, nor orders to tell us what to do. At length we discovered the truth of the matter. The enemy had cut all our telegraphic wires. We were quite isolated on our hilltop ; and though we tried to pick up our friends by heliograph we never succeeded in getting them. Meanwhile we lay there, a small detachment, and a most admirable prey for the enemy's enterprise. If they had known where we were and thought it worth while, they could easily have cut us off and wiped out the whole remains of the battalion. I suppose that they did not know that we were there. Indeed, in the tangles of this country a great army might lie hidden for weeks. I reflected that if we were to be caught in a trap I would as soon be with the Punjabis as any regiment in the country. Most of them were Sikhs, and though many Sikhs have degenerated, becoming lazy and dirty and fond of liquor, they are not men who will lightly surrender, at any rate, to a Mohammedan enemy.

How it was that we were not discovered by the Germans it is hard to imagine, for our lack of rations forced us to send messages to the surrounding villages asking for foodstuffs, mealie-meal, and cattle, to be sent into the camp for purchase at fair prices. The villagers came most readily, telling us that little had been left to them by the Germans, who had pillaged all their *shambas* and driven their cattle away. And though a good many of these things may have been said with the idea of humouring us, the new invaders, I am inclined to think that they spoke the truth ; for later, when we lay waiting in front of the mountains at Kanga, we found that hordes of Masai in war-paint were scouring the

country behind us and making free with isolated
German farms to repay themselves for the cattle,
their only wealth, which they had lost at the hands
of the enemy.

The inhabitants of these small villages near Kilimanjaro came to us without fear. They brought
us sacks of mealie flour, cakes of the country tobacco,
milk with the acrid flavour of the gourd, and a few
small sheep of the Abyssinian kind which had escaped
the Germans' notice. Of vegetables or fruit they had
none. Indeed the whole of this country is almost
without cultivated fruits. For their milk we paid
them six cents (or a penny) a bottle; for the mealie-
meal a penny a pound; for the sheep two rupees
(two and eightpence) each; and for a chicken a
quarter of a rupee. But they could not, or would
not, sell us as much as we wanted, even though they
seemed eager to get hold of our silver. It was here
that we met for the first time the new German paper
currency, notes of five rupees printed on a rough,
greenish paper, and also their *heller* pieces made
from used Mauser cartridge-cases. Only a few of
these villagers were allowed inside of our perimeter,
though we had no assurance that these few were not
spies. They gathered in a semicircle under a great
tree, and here the officer commanding the Twenty-

ninth, held a kind of *indaba* at which the prices to be given for all these foods were settled. A solemn and unemotional people they seemed, with something of the Arab's dignity, and wearing the long robes of spotless linen which the coastal natives affect ; and when they spoke I noticed that they were using an inflected Swahili nearer to the classical type of the language which is spoken in Zanzibar. But we were still at least seventy miles from the coast.

With the milk which they brought in their gourds I was able to feed my new invalids, and save a little for myself ; but my principal purchase was a small serval kitten, a fluffy creature, spotted like a leopard, all teeth and claws and spitting malice or rather, to do the little thing justice, fear. There were three of them which the villagers brought to our *indaba*. A few nights before one of the villages had wakened to a great commotion, and found the mother cat dragging away a kid from their flock. In a moment she had been pierced by half a dozen slender spears, and then they had gone to sleep again and thought no more about it. But in the morning, just outside their *boma*, they had found three small spotted kittens, huddled together for the sake of warmth and crying for food. A funny little cry, like the

chirping of sparrows. One of these I bought for a
rupee and I called her Billi, which is the *Urdu* for
cat. She was a savage little creature, for many days
hostile and inconsolable, and I feared she would
have died of starvation, for she would not feed and
could not learn to lap, though she would gnaw at
my finger with her needle teeth until it bled.

Of me she was afraid, but all black flesh she des-
perately hated, finding in it, I suppose, the smell of
her hereditary enemy. It was several weeks before
she lost her savage fear, and even her play was a
little violent ; but in the end she came to depend
on me for everything, and would cry like a sparrow
at night to be taken up on to my blankets to sleep.
She was a beautifully clean little animal with little
of the wild cat's smell about her.

We had lain at Kilimanjaro three days when headquarters sent a motor cyclist to us with an order,
twenty-four hours old, to join in the combined
attack upon Handeni. All the time we had been
in view of the great conical hill which overhangs
that station, and an officer of the intelligence department, who had ridden in with fever, had told me
how he had stolen up to the *boma*, a stone castel-
lated building, surrounded by askaris' barracks,
and set in the middle of vast plantations of rubber

and fields of sisal hemp.   The German flag, he said, was still flying from the tower of the castle.   The part of the Punjabis in this manœuvre, now presumably finished, was to have been the occupation of Handeni Hill.   Even though it seemed rather late in the day a double company was sent out to effect this, while the rest of us marched out of Kilimanjaro in the direction of Endarema, where it was believed that the trolley line ended, and three great military roads converged.

The day was very hot.   My ambulance wagons had not yet been returned by the division, and so my sick men were obliged to walk ; for though I borrowed a couple of empty A.T. carts from the Punjabis' transport officer, the going in the sandy soil was too hard for the bullocks, and we had to turn them out again ; but in a while we emerged from the woods, and leaving the sandy crown of the hills, found ourselves upon a fine road with a surface of hard earth running right under the base of Handeni Hill itself. It was not strange that the sight of this road encouraged us, for it was the first permanent highway that we had seen since we left Taveta, two hundred miles away, and the mere fact of such a way existing implied a degree of civilisation which we had not met before.   It promised stone houses and gardens, fruit and vegetables and fresh milk, all the things of which we had almost forgotten the taste. It is strange how the mind of the soldier must dwell upon food—by far the most important matter in his daily life.

Indeed we were not disappointed, for the red road breasting a hill revealed to us such a sight as we had not seen for months—a wide basin of country ringed by mountains which showed on every side tokens of cultivation. As a matter of fact, about Handeni there are not many farms. There is one great rubber estate which covers many miles, and it was the fresh green of the rubber plantations with their ordered uniformity which was so pleasing to our eyes, so different, so very different, from the endless ashen grey of the bush. Here too were trim native *bandas*, thrusting their pointed roofs above the paler green of mealie-fields. And here was a red road, no uncertain track which might shortly lose itself in the bush, but one that ran straight forward, as with a gay confidence, into a country that was known and tamed and civilised. In a little while, over a valley on our left, we saw the battlements of the *boma* and a flag flying. But the flag was not a tricolour. Evidently we were too late for fighting.

We learned, as we marched in, that the force

reserve, the 5th and 6th South African Infantry, had made something of a success, having caught the retreating enemy to the south-west of Handeni, and handled him roughly in a short brush. This was the first time in the Pangani trek that these regiments were in action.

The rest of the division had by this time found a camping-ground a little above the terminus of the trolley railway at Endarema ; and it was there that we joined them, moving in through the middle of the rubber plantations and crossing at last a little permanent stream spanned by a wooden bridge. A group of miserable African porters, horribly emaciated, watched us go past. Our own porters spoke with them, and we soon heard it whispered that all the water here was bad, and that dysentery was everywhere. All the land in the neighbourhood of the trolley station was horribly littered with the refuse of the German askaris, and suggested nothing in the world but squalor and disease. On our right a long shed, in which lay two hundred Africans, left by the Germans to die, was ominously labelled ' Typhus.' These sick men were mostly labourers who had been working under great pressure on the lines over which the enemy had so cleverly managed to retreat : but in the end there must have been something of a panic, for in one place, down by the wooden bridge, I found a collection of more than thirty identity disks which the coolies had thrown away, rather than be found with anything German about them. That appalling hospital—it had been left in charge of a fat farmer with a great red cross on his arm—became something of an anxiety to us. The enemy never hesitated to abandon their sick to our care when they found it difficult to feed them. It was for this reason that they left their women and children at Wilhelmstal.

The station itself had been destroyed by fire, and the trucks, having served their purpose, lay overturned with their bearings shattered. When we marched past the sheds were still smouldering, but the stationmaster's cottage of whitewashed mud was intact, and in front of it the A.P.M. sat behind a table to which the neighbouring natives were bringing poultry and eggs and vegetable produce, and this promised well for us. It was now many weeks since we had tasted any fresh food, and many of our malarial patients were developing a condition of scurvy which was due, in part, to the want of it. We were told that we might now look forward to a fortnight's rest ; that even if we were fit to advance ourselves the supplies could not possibly keep up

with us. The news came as a great relief, for, to
tell the truth, the brigade was in a bad way. The
Rhodesians were by now at less than half strength.
In a single day our ambulance admitted over seven
per cent. of the whole force.   Now, it seemed, we had
a chance of pulling things together and staying a
little while on that open hilltop among the rubber
plantations. We should get fresh food. We should
receive our mails. Perhaps we might be joined by
reinforcements. All our tired troops were grateful.
That night we slept for the first time with no thought
for the morrow.

CHAPTER XVII

S<small>UCH</small> were our hopes, but at dawn next morning a messenger brought me orders to take a light section with me to the 2nd Kashmir Rifles (Col. Lyall), who were to march within an hour to make good the Morogoro road, which threatened the flank of General Beves's column that had managed to get on to another track at the time of their Pongwe engagement. In this there was nothing to wonder at, for the most detailed maps with which we were supplied did not even state the exact position of Handeni, a place of some military importance, and the roads which radiated from this point had only been made since the beginning of the war, with a purely military object.

We were told to draw rations for three days, even though it was probable that we should not be away from Handeni more than two. Then, when this little job was over, we should take our rest with the others. The whole of the movement had been suddenly planned. The first of the Kashmiris had left Endarema before my orders arrived, and I found it impossible to get my unit in marching order, to collect the mules which had been scattered grazing in a deep valley, and take my place behind the last of them. In haste, and in some confusion, we marched out over the wooden bridge. We passed the typhus hospital, climbing that red road through the plantation by which we had come in the day before. Half-way up the hill we cut off to the right, in an alley between rubber-trees, towards the German *boma*, at which the units comprising the flying column were to meet.

Two miles or more we marched through these green plantations.

At the bottom of a little valley, where a trickle of water ran, I found a small but fertile garden in which French beans, asparagus, and tall globe artichokes were growing. It was evident that no Indian troops had passed that way, or else the place would have been stripped of all its eatable green ; for vegetable food is what the Indian on active service misses most. Here, too, I picked two pocketsful of that red-leaved flower, rosella, whose fleshy bracts make a stew that is like rhubarb, but more acrid. From this valley the road rose abruptly. The rubber-trees thinned to the two rows of an avenue and we emerged into a wide, open space bounded by small battlemented buildings of stone, whitewashed and gleaming in the sun.   These were the old askari barracks, and filling the end of the alley lay the more massive structure of the *boma*, or jail, a building of pinkish stone.

In a crude sort of way the *boma* was impressive, with an air of gloomy solidity.   All the hilltop around for a hundred yards or so had been cleared, so that the building dominated the crest.   On the further side, where the governor had lived, it was whitewashed and homely, for a deep stoep ran all the length of the house, over which a fine bougainvillea sprawled, splashing the sunny whiteness with colour ; and round the drive, in a wide sweep, grew an avenue of the flamboyant-tree, whose blood-red blossoms must have been very beautiful in their season.   I have said that the *boma* dominated the hill.   From its windows one might overlook a vast expanse of country, reaching from the cool green of the surrounding plantations to darker skylines, level and fringed with trees like those of the Surrey hills, and beyond all the fantastic shapes of the N'guru Mountains, with which we were soon to be better acquainted.

In the open space before the *boma* gates the Kashmiris were waiting, small stocky fellows, Gurkhas and Dogras, whose aspect of sturdiness was increased

. . . a deep stoep . . . over which a fine bougainvillea sprawled (*p.* 196)

by the great weight and bulk of the kit which they carried, and particularly the *chhagals* of water which all of them had slung about their shoulders. For the Gurkha is used to the running streams of Nepal, drinking whenever he pleases, and these waterless African wastes are a great trial to him. Besides the Kashmiris we had waiting for us the fine Pathans of the 17th Cavalry, and three monstrous creatures on wheels, fantastically akin in their magnitude and shape to the rhinoceros—Sir John Willoughby's cars.

In this fair morning light our column was a fine sight, and a minute later the Mountain Battery joined us, with its splendid mules and tall Sikh gunners. A gentle breeze blew from the south over these homely woodlands, and strained the Union Jack which flew from the *boma's* flagstaff. Motionless on the tower, cut out against the sky in which the flag was flying, stood a sentry, an askari of the King's African Rifles. Oh, here, at any rate, were some tangible tokens of success.

We had still a little while to wait ; and so I walked round to the shady garden at the back of the *boma*, and the long verandah of the governor's house. Evidently the family had left in a hurry. On the stoep were many empty bookcases ; but they had

left behind very few books except a complete edition
of Goethe in forty volumes, and a few children's
school-books.   Among these, strangely enough, I
found Lamb's *Tales from Shakespeare*, with a pom-
pous introduction in German.   Lamb is described
as ' ein Freund des Dichters Coleridge ' . . . a good
introduction, at which Elia himself would not have
grumbled, but hardly necessary in these days.   I
remembered the passion of Coleridge for German
philosophy.   On the flyleaf of the book was written
in a simple girlish hand the name of ' Lena Weiss,'
and I began suddenly to wonder what it must have
felt like to the family of Weiss—if indeed it was they
who lived there—to leave their flowery garden and
the pleasant, ordered homeliness of the Handeni
plantations, and fly, post haste, to Morogoro, with
our army swarming in the rear, leaving these pathetic
little evidences of their aspirations to our own culture
behind them.   For, looking at the Goethe books, I
became more than usually aware of the old, simple,
sentimental Germany, the Germany of Schumann's
lieder ; and I wondered if perhaps in these remoter
regions of the colonies there might not be many
elderly people to whom the ideals of modern Germany
were alien and repulsive—people who had never
read Von Hoffmannsthal or listened to Strauss and

Schönberg, being content with Goethe in forty volumes, and the gentle prose of Lamb. A torn magazine cover lay under my feet, printed in fantastic Gothic characters : *Kolonie und Heimath im Wort und Bild.* How very German! The very initial capitals of these high-sounding abstractions seemed typical of the national illusions. And then I picked up a medicine bottle with a poison label on it : not merely the word *Gift* in red letters, but a crudely violent print of skull and crossbones. Could any symbolism have been less subtle or more childish? That label summarised for me the whole theory of *Shrecklichkeit* in war.

First the armoured cars moved off, with an opened exhaust as loud as their machine-guns ; behind them came the Kashmiris, and the Mountain Battery ; behind the battery mules marched my stretcher-bearers. But midday is no pleasant time to start a long march in the neighbourhood of the Equator ; and though the surface of this war-road was admirable, and the dust vexed us little, the way led between walls of bush unusually dense even for this part of Africa, and in the closed space between, the wind which had pleasantly fluttered the flag on the ramparts of the *boma*, never reached us. All the morning I had moved about

o

with the unsatisfactory feeling of tiredness which
follows a badly broken night ; and so, instead of
walking, as was my habit, at the head of my
stretcher-bearers and on their windward side, I rode
the mule Simba.   It was evident to me from the
state of men and sweating beasts that the morning
was unusually hot, but I, for some strange reason,
shivered in my saddle.   I didn't realise, just at
first, that I had fever on me, the direct result of my
night in the nullah near M'kalamo, when the sepoy
Kurban Hussein had unwound his *pagri* to serve me
as covering and utterly inadequate mosquito-net.
But when, after three hours' marching we made a
little halt and I took my temperature, I found that
it was a hundred and four.   Malignant sub-tertian,
the fever which the Pangani breeds, is no small affair
in a first attack, as I knew well enough from my
experience of the young Rhodesian drafts, and so
I made no bones about retiring to my own ambulance wagon for all the sunnier part of the day.
Four times, in all, I travelled the Morogoro road
from Handeni, and only once as a whole man, so
that all my vision of it is still tinctured with the
strange atmosphere of fever.   And I think, perhaps,
that day, June the 20th, when we were the first
to set foot on it and it had not been ground into

commonplace by the wheels of all our great lorries and the hoofs of the long awaited Mounted Brigade, gave me the strangest vision of all.

A fair red road it was, with a smooth surface of earth, and on either side a deep fosse of the kind which the Romans made, and which may still be seen, by roads straight as sword-cuts, in the heart of England. Certainly a soldiers' road : and like the Roman roads in another way—in that it had been driven from strategic point to point through an utterly savage country. All the way we were expecting to spring land mines, yet nothing that was not normal happeñed in our first day's travelling of that straight road. The whole march was of an absolute uniformity, with the same grey-green thickets of thorn, waterless, and haunted by the melancholy hornbills, the same red road beneath, the same hot sky above.

Throughout the day we saw no water, nor any signs of it, until, in the evening, we came to the pit of a deep valley, some fifteen miles upon our way, with the dried-up bed of a stream around which were clustered a fine plantation of bananas, stripped, as usual, of their fruit, and several patches of pale green maize. This valley was of a fresh and exotic beauty, being all etherealised by the yellow evening

sun which made the hot air amber as at home, but
of a peculiar and paler clarity.   Here, too, rose one
of those silvery trees whose trunks are smooth as a
fine pillar, unbroken by any branch beneath the
expanded crown, and gleaming with a lustre as of
satin.   I could well understand that any heathen
should have worshipped this great and lovely creature ; for indeed it was the genius of that place, and
all the rest of the valley seemed to have been there
only for the use of ministering to its loveliness.   We
crossed the pit of the valley, and climbed the further
hill, right beneath the bole of this giant, which
divided in splendid flutings to clasp the earth.   I
suppose it was more beautiful, this tree, because it
rose straight against a dark hillside rather than
against the sky.

Half-way up the slope colour parties were called
for.   It had been decided to halt upon the hill above
the great tree for the night, for there was a waterhole in the valley, and waterholes were so rare, and
so uncertain at the best of times, that it would have
been foolish to pass it by.   The position, too, was a
fine one from a military point of view, being the
stony crown of a hill, with a narrow ridge towards
the enemy on one side, and on the others the road,
with its fosse, and the valley of the stream.   But the

First the armoured cars moved off, with an open exhaust as loud as their machine-guns (p. 203)

ascent was troublesome, and our tired mules, which
were by now no more than skeletons, faced it with
difficulty. At the last they jibbed, and crack went
the disselboom of one of my ambulance wagons. The
only thing   could do was to leave it there in the
road, as far to the side as possible, while we out-
spanned the beasts and kept them in reserve for the
other wagons. For we knew that before long our
mules would be dying wholesale. Already more
than one of them showed that slight puffiness beneath
the chest which is one of the first signs of trypanosomiasis. The very road upon which we left the
ambulance swarmed that night with biting tsetse-
flies.

I was unfeignedly thankful that the day's march
was at an end, for now my body burned like a
furnace. I managed to get round to Colonel Lyall's
headquarters for orders, and was told that we should
not march before daybreak. I wrapped myself up
in as many blankets as I could find, and tried to
sleep. I suppose I did sleep, for next day I seemed
to remember many dreams, in one of which, a thing
of horror, I was condemned to walk the dry bush
eternally, so that I prayed for death and at last
found it with thankfulness. And also I remember,
in one dream, how my servant who had wandered

off into a small village, brought me a fowl ; and how, when I asked him how much he had given for it, he replied ' Nothing,' which meant either that I was dreaming or that he was a thief. But darkness had hardly fallen in its velvety completeness when there came to my dreaming or waking ears the sound of firing : at first a few isolated shots, and then the continuous stutter of machine-guns, rising from a sullen spite—as if it were really too late to have disturbed them—to a state of violent irritation. Somewhere—it seemed to me due west—our troops were heavily engaged. I threw aside my blankets and picked my way among the scattered rocks to headquarters. At the top of the rise I could hear the firing no longer. A comfortable staff captain said that some one else had heard a noise ' of sorts,' but was convinced that it was only the battery mules stamping. They were going to think no more about it. And I was bound to confess that on their side of the crest the firing—for I still knew that it was firing—was hard to hear. But when I came back to my own camp it was clearer than ever, and the Kavirondos had stopped chattering and eating to listen.

I rolled myself up in my blankets again and tried to sleep. Now the stretcher-bearers were quite

quiet, like starlings at nightfall. Above me stretched
the branches of a great tree moving so gently that
one who was not watching would have thought them
still ; but between them fixed stars were shining
with a pulsing flame, and by these I could see how
softly they were stirred. Of course I could not
sleep. That is the worst of fever. For an hour or
more I heard the angry maxim fire waxing and
waning, and then all was quiet. All was quiet
except my fevered brain. A lot of half-remembered
poetry went singing through it :

> ' In the moonlight the shepherds,
> Soft lulled by the rills,
> Lie wrapped in their blankets
> Asleep on the hills.
>
> Not here. O Apollo !
> Are haunts meet for thee. . . .'

I believe I had got the lines in the wrong order, but
the overwhelming reasonableness of illogical nonsense was quite in keeping with my night. I dreamed
(or perhaps I didn't dream) some verses, which
however feeble they may have been, were as little
of my conscious brain's making as the mighty Kubla
Khan.

' Kubla Khan,' I mused in my waking. ' From his
name I should imagine he's a Pathan . . . perhaps

in the 130th Baluchis, or the 40th. But here we have only Kashmiris . . . so *that* can't be right. And yet the name. . . . A funny business.'

This is what the fever made for me in that rich darkness at the camp on the stony hill above the big tree :

When I lay fevered yesternight
My fever's flame was a clear light,
A taper, flaring in the wind,
Whither, fluttering out of the dim
Night, many dreams glimmered by :
Like moths out of the darkness, blind
Hurling at the taper's flame,
From drinking honey of the night's flowers
Into my circled light they came,
So near, I could see their soft colours,
Grey of the dove, most soothly grey,
But the heat singed their wings, and away
Darting into the dark again
They escaped me . . .
                    Others floated down
Like those vaned seeds that fall
In Autumn from the sycamore's crown,
When no leaf trembleth, nor branch is stirred,
More silent in flight than any bird
Or bat's wings flitting in darkness ; soft
As lizards moving on a white wall
They came quietly from aloft
Down through my circle of light, and so
Into unlighted gloom below . . .
        But one dream, strong-winged, daring,
Flew beating at the heart of the flame,

Till I feared it would have put out my light—
My thin taper, fitfully flaring—
And that I should be left alone in the night
With no more dreams for my delight.

Can it be, that from the dead
Even their dreams, their dreams are fled?

It was only midnight.   H——, the staff captain, wakened me.

' We start in an hour's time,' he said.   ' Yes . . . orders from G.H.Q.   Beves has been getting it all right.'

The stars no longer shone between the branches of the tree.   The night was very cold, and great clouds drooped upon us.

CHAPTER XVIII

THE battery mules stumbled over the smooth stones. For it was very dark under that low sky, and upon so secret a mission we could use no lights. My own mule, Simba, lunged up against one of them, and got kicked for his pains. In the darkness the column took a long time disentangling itself from the convolutions of the perimeter camp, and we left behind us the cavalry and the armoured cars, who could move faster and catch us up even if they did not start before daybreak.

We emerged upon the hillside road a good hundred yards above the place where I had left my broken wagon. Against the cloudy darkness we could see a great number of pointed roofs shaped like bee-hives, and then, with an almost startling effect, a long tin shanty with a wooden cross above its eastern end. It was a German mission-house, deserted, of course, and not only deserted, but deliberately fouled by their askaris. I suppose the idea was to deprive us of any comfort which they might leave behind; this was not the only place in which the same thing had been done; but this descent from the broad

203

principles of frightfulness to the childish and filthy detail was a useless and disgusting procedure which an English mind finds it difficult to explain. The smell of the place was abominable, and I think it hung more heavily in the air because the atmosphere itself was flat and still, as though we had happened upon an hour when all that swarming green-stuff was expiring its dead air. And then as we passed the crest it began to rain—the last thing in the world we might have expected at this time of the year, a heavy, beating rain that quickly soaked us through And I knew that this rain must mean a new outbreak of fever for many of us.

So I rode on, for, aching as I was, I felt that the swaying walk of Simba would be more tolerable, if only because it was regular, than the jolting of an ambulance wagon.

We moved very slowly, for we thought that the two roads must converge in a little while, and indeed the firing overnight had not sounded very far away. We expected to bump the enemy at any moment, and four miles further at the most. Ahead of us the Gurkhas, flanking our advance, moved slowly through the mealie-fields and we, upon the road, marched between monstrous dead stalks that rattled in the rain. For an hour we marched. For

two hours. The rain had done us one good turn, for
it had laid the dust. Looking ahead we reflected
that when daylight came there would be no rufous
column in the sky to tell the enemy when our
armoured cars and the cavalry and the transport
were coming.

Out of the mealie-fields we passed into a country
of open bush. A sudden valley dipped before us,
and then, on our left, a great pinnacle of rock, shagged
with dark trees, pushed its shadow into the clouds.
A fine position, we thought . . . they could have
made of it a second Salaita. We halted a little, and
then, most cautiously, moved forward.

And now the road, descending, cut into the heart
of a great forest, of a kind which we hadn't seen
before. The trees stood up very straight and tall,
and the whole wood gave a sense of spaciousness
and freedom, for they did not grow very close
together, and the undergrowth about their boles was
scanty, being mostly a pale, fine grass. By this time
we had surely advanced more than four miles, and
as yet there was no sign of the meeting of the roads,
nor even of the enemy. We couldn't understand
it ; for by now we must be very near to the scene
of last night's fighting. Again we waited. Patrols
reached out ahead of us a long way and returned

reporting nothing but the same thin forest of straight trees. Being in this doubt we received an order to fall out in the grass at the side of the road under the shelter of the trees. And there, propped against a felled trunk I lay, shivering, till dawn showed a yellow light through the clerestory of the forest where the treetops were shagged with a trailing parasite of silvern grey like immense tangled cobwebs.

With the first light we heard behind us a sound as of distant maxim fire, and stood to arms. It was the armoured cars arriving. They came lumbering past in the pride of their strength and invulnerability. And still we did not move.

A little later a reserve officer of the 17th Cavalry cantered up. He rode damnably, and when he reached my level asked me who we were. 'How long have you been halted here?' he asked: and when I told him two or three hours he seemed surprised. 'Why, you 've only come a couple of miles since midnight,' he said. It was hard to believe, but we had marched very slowly 'And you 've been ordered to halt?' 'Yes.' 'Well, I 've no orders,' he said, 'and so I think we 'd better stay where we are.'

At last we moved on This forest country was very beautiful in its way: but as the sun climbed the

sky the heat became intense, and I learned again
how the parasite of malaria seems to revel in the
sunshine. I would have been thankful now for a
lift in the ambulance, but we had left all our wheeled
transport behind, and I had to make the best I
could of Simba, struggling out of my saddle to lie
down in the grass at the wayside whenever a halt
was called. And these were many, because our way
was still extremely uncertain. Nor was I any the
better for my laborious descents, for while I lay
aching in the grass my knees were smothered with
fat ticks. I was almost too tired to worry about
pulling them off.

All that morning we marched on, and still no sign
of Beves. It was early afternoon when we reached
a muddy stream, running in a cleft between the
hills. On our right a thin wood of resinous trees
climbed a steep slope, and when we halted there
we quickly saw that many branches had been shorn
away, and the trunks scarred by the flight of bullets.
The grazes and gashes in the trees were still exuding
a juice of the colour of blood, and beneath them all
the ground was trampled and the grasses bent. We
knew at once that this must have been the scene
of the engagement which we had heard, and yet it
was hard to believe, for we must have marched at

least fourteen miles, and the firing had seemed to us very much nearer than this. I suppose some strange conformation in the shapes of the hills, or peculiar condition of the air must have brought the battle nearer to us. We learned, afterwards, that the firing had been heard at Handeni, many miles further away. And then we heard that Beves was in front of us, having hit the road at this point instead of at the junction of the two, on the night before, and that all this time he had been wondering what had happened to us.

The troops which had been engaged in this affair were, once more, the 5th South African Infantry. We felt sorry for the 5th; for this business seemed to balance their success at Pongwe three days before.

It happened this way. The Germans had evidently been expecting our forces to advance by their bigger road, the 'autoweg,' the way which we had followed. The accidental advance of the South Africans along the other road, which, in spite of its very fair surface, they labelled a 'fussweg,' took them by surprise, and rather an uncomfortable surprise, for they had already settled the exact point on the Morogoro road at which they might let fly at us, had prepared their fields of fire by felling trees, and concealed with admirable earthworks the guns which were to mow us down. Nor only this, for all along the road in the rear of their position they had dug rifle-pits and other machine-gun emplacements, so that they might keep up a running fight during the retirement for which they were prepared. The appearance of the South Africans on the footway upset all their plans. Always, so far, the retreating Germans had been able to choose the conditions under which they should meet us, and they intended this fight to be no different. And so, Kraut's skirmishers, meeting the South African advance-guard on the footway, lightly engaged them, and, always keeping touch, retreated—but retreated always in the direction of the motorway to eastward where their maxims and pom-poms were waiting. And behind them came an unlucky company of the 5th. I say ' unlucky,' but I think they had more fortune than their prudence deserved ; for it happened that a nervous German askari discharged a rifle when they were some distance from the position. Otherwise they would have marched straight on to it, and not only they but the rest of the regiment would have suffered. As it was, the company lost a hundred men, and partly by reason of their own dogged courage in sticking, one after another, to their machine-gun, which had been planted by a tree that had been accurately ranged, and was swept continually by the enemy's fire.

All these things happened after sunset, and to judge from the scars which high branches of the trees revealed, the shooting of the askaris must have become very wild. Even in this bush warfare, where man, one would think, is matched against single man, the machine-gun has become the most important weapon. That is partly the reason why the Germans in this campaign have been able to put up so splendid a resistance.

It was some consolation to us to know that even if we had been nearer we could not very well have helped in this encounter. If, on the other hand, the South Africans had not been diverted from their original road and had marched on, leaving us to follow up along the motorway, the Germans would never have been able to use their position, but would have been forced to retire or be caught between us. And I think if there is any blame to be taken for the fact that this didn't happen, it must be laid upon the character of the country; for though we were not many miles from Beves (though more than we imagined) as the crow flies, it would have taken at least a day to find out where he was by the method of pushing out patrols to get in touch with him.

P

We left the scene of that engagement and pushed
on another four miles, through a hilly country
clothed in the same sparse forest, coming at last to
the junction of the roads, where a Gothic finger-post
stood : and there, in the midst of the forest, and
underneath its shade, we made an entrenched camp
astride of both ways, and looked forward to our
promised rest.   But when next day came there was
no talk of this, nor even of a return to Handeni.
We heard instead that the whole brigade was moving
out from Endarema that day, and might be expected
to make in three days the point which we had reached
in two.

Our own first concern was water.   Below us, on
the further side of the footway, ran a little glade in
the forest, full of rank grass which looked as if it
might collect the moisture of the slopes on either
side.   There was no stream, nor any sign of one ;
but here we digged a series of deep pits, and found
that for a space of two feet or so beneath the surface
mould, black moisture trickled from the earth.   This
water was thicker than coffee and we had not enough
alum to precipitate the solid matter in any quantity,
so we made many of these pits, and after they had
filled, we allowed the water in them to stand and
settle for a day, after which, even if it were not

palatable, the taste of leaf mould might be mitigated with tea. It was not, however, the quality but the quantity of this water which concerned me, for the surface area was small, and I feared that it might be exhausted even before the brigade arrived. How I could prepare a water supply for four thousand men, Heaven only knew. Evidently we were expected to stay here, for on the second day the colonel of the Kashmiris had built himself a *banda*.

But on that second day, N——, of the Intelligence Department, came in to me with a couple of German prisoners, miserable, dejected creatures suffering from dysentery ; and while I gave him a meal, he told me that he had been riding out behind the German lines ; that several companies were happily encamped about four miles ahead of us, and others a little further back. ' The country isn't really so bad,' he said, ' and I don't see why we shouldn't scupper the lot. It 's simply a matter of speed.'

He told me that he was going straight back with his report to Smuts. ' And I don't think he 'll let the chance go,' he said.

A very modest fellow, N——. I had always a great respect for these few men of the I. D. who carried their lives in their hands so gallantly.

CHAPTER XIX

WE had not long to wait. Next day we heard that
the whole division had moved up to Kangata, the
scene of the South Africans' affair, and were encamped above that muddy water. The same afternoon the Kashmiris moved on, leaving with me
close on a hundred sick with fever. I thought that
I should have moved with the regiment, but orders
came for me to stay by the forking of the roads
until the brigade should overtake me. The move
of the Kashmiris was both sudden and secret. I
doubt if the enemy at M'zinga knew that they had
gone ; for they went no further along the road but
cut off nearly due west. It was clear that Smuts
was acting, swiftly as usual, on N——'s intelligence.
Perhaps, too, he thought it well to put some more
heart into the South Africans as an antidote to
Kangata.

This was the strategy of our new movement. The
enemy, as N—— had told me, lay with an advanced
post at M'zinga on the Morogoro road (our ' autoweg ') ; and larger forces, in support, with their
heavy artillery towards the Lukigura river, a stream

of unknown magnitude, but certainly a formidable obstacle in the rains. The bulk of Kraut's northern army was believed to be in front of the bridgehead ; and southward, beyond the river, loomed those blue masses of the N'guru Mountains, fertile and well watered, which overhung and commanded the military road to Morogoro and the Central Railway, the obvious channel of our invasion. Once established in these tangled hills, a tract of some twelve hundred square miles (or, say, twice the size of Dartmoor), well equipped, and able to live on the fertile land, the enemy would be difficult to dislodge. It was therefore decided to make an attempt to cut off the forces north of the Lukigura ; and to this end the Kashmiris who had started in the afternoon, and the divisional troops under General Hoskins, who had left Kangata earlier in the day, were to march all night through the forest to westward, cross the Lukigura in its upper waters, and descend upon the bridgehead from the right bank.

Little was known of the country through which this march must be made. For some part of it, at any rate, the same thin forest, with its gentle valleys and rough grass, covered the land. But it was known that the country sloped gently in the main towards the river, and whatever tangles of forest

or acacia might be encountered, the flanking force
might be expected to cross the stream by noon on
the next day.   Meanwhile, the usual spear-head, the
First Brigade, was to march with as much speed and
show as possible along the Morogoro road to start
a holding action which might divert the enemy's
attention from the other secret move, and to bring
full pressure to bear on them only when we were
certain that the others were in their rear.

The brigade arrived without warning, so suddenly
that my unit held up the Rhodesian rearguard for a
few minutes ; for the mules were all out grazing and
the Cape-boys had to find them and drive them in.
It was nearly dark when we started, and the way
seemed long, although we cannot have marched
many miles.   But the fever was still on me, and
three days of high temperature do not leave a man
at his best.   Our halts were many, the way uncertain,
and the transport even more troublesome than
usual.

At length, from darkness and confusion, we passed
into a most unusual light.   The brigade had fallen
out to bivouac on the right of the road, in a patch
of woodland like that through which we had been
passing in everything except that it was more full
of tripping undergrowth and thorn.   Along the road

the Rhodesians had lighted many fires : evidently it was intended that the enemy should know where we were, or at any rate that they should fix their attention on our obvious approach to the exclusion of the flanking column, the South Africans, the Kashmiris, the Lancs, and the Fusiliers, now streaming silently through the night over the hills to the westward. All the time that I saw those fires of ours I thought of the others and of their secret progress.

I had never seen a more disordered bivouac than that. I suppose that it was not thought worth while to camp with any method for so short a time ; and when we had eaten, and put our beasts to graze, we lay down about our red fires, and snatched what sleep we could before the rising of the moon. At three o'clock we pushed off. In the narrow way it was difficult to find our proper station. The road was full of mules kicking and plunging in the dark. Our usual companions, the Mountain Battery, had gone off with the Kashmiris, and instead of them we had for neighbours the fifth battery of South African Field Artillery, quick-firing fourteen-pounders that had never yet been in action and were burning for the opportunity. But this was no sort of country for the gunners.

When once we were started the going was fairly

easy, as it must have been if our animals were to live ; the last few days had seen so many mules and horses die. We crossed a steep hill and came suddenly upon an enormous bonfire. The Germans moving only a little before us had destroyed a great store of petroleum tins, many hundreds of them, by fire. There were so many that forty hours later, when I passed the spot once more, the heap was still flaring. In the middle of the road lay an abandoned Ford car, with its front axle smashed, and for at least two hundred feet along the right of our path stretched a great grass-roofed *banda*, that was now in danger of catching fire from the flames of paraffin. I think it would have been no bad business if this had happened, for the *banda* was one which had been used, with a host of others, to house the German askaris. I have never happened on a stench so foul as that which arose from this deserted barracks. I suppose the Germans had guessed that they would not stay at M'zinga for long, and had therefore thought it was not worth while to think of sanitation. But we were thankful when we had passed that village.

It was now daybreak, and in that cool time we passed on through a pleasant country, sloping gently towards the south. The road ran for the greater part of the way in a natural depression, with wooded slopes and grassy glades on either side, from either of which a sniper might have commanded it; but in these early hours of the morning we were not troubled by them at all. Through this we marched till the sun had come to his strength, when the whole column seemed to slacken its pace. It was important, as we realised, that we should not force the Germans to fall back on the Lukigura before the other force arrived. We moved slowly and silently, as we always did when we were expecting the rattle of maxims to break out in front. It was somewhat surprising when the expected sound came from our rear—three distinct rifle shots, which turned out to be no more than the motor cycle of a dispatch rider misfiring !

But we had not long to wait for the real thing. In a few moments rifle fire began in front, and almost at once the machine-guns joined in. A minute later a shell sang over our heads, echoing mightily in that close valley, with a high screaming note that was new to us. It came, I think, from one of the small quick-firers of the Gatling model, which the Germans call a revolver gun, and we misnamed a pom-pom.

Now the fighting became fairly vigorous in front. The armoured cars were in action, while we, with the artillery, were halted in the hollow behind, and feeling very much out of it. This was the first time that Willoughby's cars had been engaged, and we were curious to know what would happen to them ; for though they looked formidable enough, with a maxim fore and aft, it seemed to us that any wheeled thing ran the risk of being immobilised and taken. What actually happened was this. The first car, moving ponderously down the road, suddenly found itself on the brink of a four-foot trench, the Germans' obvious reply to this sort of engine. It pulled up sharp, and immediately received a pom-pom shell in the radiator. The range cannot have been more than fifty yards, and the aim was admirable, for the shell struck the radiator exactly in the space between the opened louvres. It speaks well for the handling of this car that in a few moments its drivers had put it to rights, filled in the trench and got it going again, besides bringing their machine-gun into action.

This was the beginning of the fight at Lukigura river. But things developed slowly. We were not anxious to make a strong attack before we were certain that the other column had crossed the river. All the time we were waiting for the sound of their fire. And it was now noon, and nothing had been heard of them. Waiting behind the crest of the hill for nearly an hour of suspense, we suddenly became aware of shapes of men moving along the skyline on our left in the direction of our rear, moving in quick starts from cover to cover. It occurred to us at once that we might be in for a repetition of the rush at M'kalamo, and we sent a message forward to the main body and back to the rearguard at once, while a small party of Rhodesians, who were guarding the South African field-guns, cut off into the bush towards the skyline along which they had passed. A message back from the front assured us that the ridge was held by our pickets : but, almost as soon, another arrived from the rear asking for an ambulance to fetch a number of men who had been hit by snipers. A determined little attack had been made on the transport of the brigade, and most of the drivers had taken to the bush. At the same moment an order came for the guns to advance, and we followed them.

And now, far to the southward, heavy firing began, and we knew that the flanking column had got in touch with the enemy. On the brow of the hill we were checked again, immediately behind the big Vauxhall in which Smuts daily risked his life. The general was standing there, talking happily and faster than usual, to his chief of staff.   I had never seen him so obviously pleased with himself.   Evidently things were going well.   They had been examining a captured German askari, and what he had told them had pleased the commander-in-chief.

' He says they don't mind shell fire or machine-guns very much, but they can't stand " the bird." '

That is what they call our aeroplanes.

' He says that when they see " the bird " coming they run for their lives into the bush.   The askaris who drag the big guns about are chained to them for that reason.   They 'll go anywhere rather than face " the bird." . . . He says this Lukigura river is full of crocodiles, but they 'd go into that to get away from " the bird."   We must give them some more of " the bird." . . . You see it isn't merely physical terror.   They think it is magic.'

By this time the flanking column was blazing away in front.   The guns were unlimbered and a field of fire cleared before their muzzles.   This was going to be the chance of the patient South African gunners. Every moment they were busy taking fresh ranges. But in the end they never fired a shot, for the whole of that shelving river valley was clogged with dense bush, and we could never be sure that we were not peppering our own men with shrapnel.   Down in that

bush the enemy were having a rough time of it.
General Hoskins had not been able to cross the river
as soon as we expected, for the country through
which their night march had led them had been very
difficult. Indeed, it was three o'clock in the afternoon before his troops crossed the Lukigura, and
all the firing which we had heard had been on the
left bank of the stream. At the same time there
was no doubt as to the surprise of the movement.
The principal share of the fighting fell to the 25th
Fusiliers, who cut up the best part of a German
company, and one of their best companies at that,
capturing a pom-pom and two machine-guns, and
making many prisoners. This exploit was com-
pleted by a bayonet charge, a very rare thing in
bush warfare.

While this engagement on the enemy's flank was
proceeding, the advanced troops of our own brigade,
Baluchis and Punjabis, encountered the enemy as
they tried to break away to the north-east and swept
them in the open with a very deadly maxim fire.
Altogether, in spite of our failure to get behind the
Germans, the day was most successful. The enemy
casualties can never be known, for many dead
askaris were left to rot in the thick bush and never
discovered to this day, while our own losses were less

than a fourth of the South Africans' casualties at
Kangata.   By four o'clock in the afternoon all firing
had ceased, but prisoners were still coming in, many
of them scared to death by the noise of maxim fire
in the echoing bush.   The achievement of a single
officer, and not a very big one at that, to whom eight
askaris and two white officers surrendered for the
asking, although they were all armed and he was
not, is typical of the enemy's morale at the end of
the Lukigura fight.

We dressed our wounded, and camped upon a
little ridge above the roadway.   But I could do no
more.   This was my fifth day of fever, and that
evening I found myself a patient in the British Field
Ambulance, than which nothing can be more trying
to a doctor.   I suppose our position on the ridge so
near an object of known position, in this case the
road, invited the attention of the enemy's artillery.
In the ordinary way I had not so far greatly minded
shell fire, but in this case the effect was really
rather terrifying, because I was not a whole man
ready to take my chance with the others, but sick
and badly off for nerves, lying alone with no more
cover than a flimsy tent in darkness only lit by the
tremendous flashes of the bursting shell, and shaken
by the reports which echoed through all that forest.

I do not know why it should be so, but I have
noticed time after time that the moral effect of
shell fire is greater at night, and the sound of bursting high explosive more tremendous. Perhaps it is
because when all things are asleep a great number
of small sounds which make, in the daytime, a sort
of background for the greater, are hushed, and the
detonation of a bursting shell is thrown upon absolute silence in the same way as its flash stands out
against the blackness of night. At any rate, that
night for me was one of little sleep, for in the
middle of it, another officer was brought into my
tent in the throes of dysentery.

CHAPTER XX

NEXT morning it became evident that my fate had passed out of my own control, and that it had been determined that I should be sent back. Before I was fully awake, being now only slightly feverish but a poor figure of a man none the less, I was ordered to hurry back to Handeni, on the first empty supply lorry, with some of the wounded, and there rest till I was told to come back again. The day was very hot and the lorry jolted hellishly over the nullahs, where a corduroy of branches had been spread to take the weight of our guns ; and I, who travelled with the driver under a sort of hood, felt full of pity for the poor Indians behind, for I knew how unkindly is the sun to a man with fever.

That drive back over the forty miles to Handeni —it took us seven hours—was a strange experience to me. Before this I had seen nothing of the back of the front. All my journeying had been made through a savage and hostile country, with the fear of surprise at every turning, the sense of maxims lurking in every mealie patch and enemy patrols concealed on every shoulder of rising ground. Now the whole character of the road seemed to have changed. Everywhere, even in so short a time, the romantic and adventurous atmosphere of our march had given way to the phlegmatic unconcern of ' lines of communication.' To the drivers of lorries moving over that road, places which will always live in the imagination of a few thousand men, such as that bullet-swept wood at Kangata, were no more than undistinguished pieces of a devil of a country. From the scanty water for which the South Africans had fought, as precious as King David's wasted cup, they filled their radiators. By the wood of the shaggy trees, above the water-holes, the Army Service Corps had established a refilling point. On the edge of the road a corporal sat stolidly smoking on a case of bully beef.

It took all these things to make me realise the immense force which moves behind, sustaining the intense ardours of war, ministering without any great enthusiasm to our romance, restoring the country which our fiery passage has disturbed to the flat conditions of peace. And it wasn't the organisation of these people on L. of C. that I now found myself admiring, but the patience which they must bring to bear on so dull a business as running convoys of food over roads which our fighting had made im-

Q

passable, with no excitement in the world but that of incredible rumours about the doings of other people. It made me feel very sorry for all those who were scattered the length of our enormous lines of communication, who knew neither the comforts of an office billet in a base, nor the sustained excitement of the firing line.

At Handeni one was oppressed by the same feeling of stagnation, though Hannyngton's camp on the hill opposite the *boma* gave a more dynamic aspect to the place ; but even that seemed unduly settled and peaceable, for the askaris of the K.A.R. had built themselves an elaborate village of grass *bandas*, as though they were going to live there for ever, and not only huts for themselves, but an orderly-room and a guard-room over which floated a captured German ensign at half mast.

I had been told, when I left Lukigura, to make myself a room in the *boma*. Probably, they said, you will be the only person there. But when my lorry pulled up at the gate of the jail I saw that they had been mistaken. I suppose that other people beside myself had not realised the way in which the administrative services followed hot in our footsteps. In two rooms which had once been a post-office the telegraphists had installed themselves, while the residential part of the *boma* was already chock-full of wounded South Africans from the Kangata fight. Here they were being dealt with under wretched circumstances—for they had not even stretchers to lie on—by the officers of Hannyngton's Brigade Field Ambulance, who had already expended on them the greater part of their reserve of available dressings. As for ward orderlies or other personnel, there were none available. The fact that Hannyngton's Brigade happened to be still at Handeni was a matter of pure good fortune, for if they had not been there there would have been no one to receive these casualties who had been dumped into the empty *boma*. And the nearest Casualty Clearing Station was still at German Bridge, some eighty miles away. It was now three days since the Kangata fight ; up till the next day no single medical officer could be sent forward, and even then, one only, without dressings or dressers to help him.

Here was an emergency in which, fever or no fever, I had to turn to ; and I think my days of rest at Handeni were among the busiest I spent in the whole campaign. At last, by slow degrees, the fifty-second Casualty Clearing Station (Lowland Division) arrived, with stores and dressings and a limited amount of personnel. At the same time an Indian unit moved up to take over the charge of Africans and Indian troops.

But even then things were not easy at Handeni, for the nearest supply depot from which we could draw rations for ourselves and our wounded was nearly a hundred miles away, and the divisional depot at the head of the trolley line, near Endarema, refused to supply us with food even though we were in charge of divisional sick. And this one can well understand, for the troops ahead were still on half rations, descending at one time to no more variety than biscuits of the detestable Hardman brand and biltong full of maggots. In face of the division's necessity a small collection of wounded had little claim. Gradually, however, matters righted themselves. One must not deal too hardly with the administrators of the L. and C.; for the whole of this invasion had been launched with such incredible swiftness and persistence that it would have been wonderful if they had managed to keep pace with us in our violent and sudden rushes. In the end we were tolerably well fed and had sufficient staff to deal with our patients, though, before I left it, the little cache of wounded in the Handeni *boma* had grown to be a hospital capable of holding over a thousand white

. . . the German prisoners had been sent back on empty lorries to our base (*p. 235*)

and native troops, and the German prisoners had been sent back on empty lorries to the base.

And so it came about that I had a little rest after all, though, indeed, I would far sooner have lain with the brigade at Lukigura.

On every side the campaign seemed to stagnate. Brits, the long-awaited Brits of rumour, had reached Luchomo with his Mounted Brigade, and was encamped there, losing, as we heard, an average of fifty horses a day from fly alone. It was always a puzzle to us that he should have been left for two long periods of inactivity in places which were not only found to be full of fly, but known to be fly-infested, from the German charts, long before they came to be occupied. Such were Luchomo and Lukigura, in which camps the Mounted Brigade spent over six weeks in all. Ahead of us there came no word of an advance, nor any news of excitement, unless it were the unfortunate loss of the divisional general's A.D.C. from a sniper's bullet when he and his chief were driving along a bush road in enemy country, after the daring manner of the G.O.C. himself. Hannyngton still remained static at Handeni. Smuts was at Luchomo, suffering from the almost inevitable malaria.

These were melancholy days, and I think Handeni,

for all its beauty, was a melancholy place.   All day, from the high ground on which the *boma* stood, I could see the sorrowful wooded country between us and the Lukigura river.   They were days of most oppressive weather, when the air stirred not at all, and in the bush many hornbills were calling.   And I do not think this impression was really the colour of my convalescence, for in a little while we knew what that weather meant.   Every afternoon the sky clouded heavily from the southward, and by evening was banked with such masses of black cloud that one would have thought a great storm was brewing.   And then night would fall upon the heavy skies.   But next morning no vestige of a cloud would remain.   Night after night this gathering of cloud grew more ominous, and even after dark one was aware of its imminence by reason of the pale lightning which washed the southern sky.   And at last, when the heavens had been charged to an intolerable pitch, the rain came, drenching and pitiless, for three days, bringing with it the strangest sense of physical relief.   It was only a little rain, with no relation, as far as we could learn, to the great seasonal downpours, but it made our communications worse than ever.   Motor lorries took two days to do the journey from Lukigura to Handeni, several of them being stranded, deeply sunk in the nullahs, while the worn earth road from German Bridge became utterly impassable.   And this was particularly trying because all our endeavour, in those days, had been to collect a great head of supplies which would let us march without anxiety on the Central Railway.

In this quiet life of Handeni I spent another two weeks untinged by any anxiety unless it were that sense of delay and suspension which is dangerous in war.   For the sake of the fresh milk which they would give our patients we had bought a herd of cows, some sixty head in all, and to shelter these from lions and Masai (who are even greater thieves) I had a great *boma* built on the site of a ragged mealie-field at the edge of the bush ; and here I lounged a great part of two days, listening to the hornbills over in the rubber, watching the lizards slide from stone to stone, and those quick, bright butterflies of Africa pilling the flowers of aromatic brushwood.   The Africans who were at work on my *boma* sang at their work.   They would climb one of the small trees of the bush, hacking with their *pangas* until every branch was stripped from it, and when a branch fell with a rending sound they would laugh together, as if this toil beneath a brazen

sky were the jolliest thing in the world. Or sometimes, when they were feeding or talking together,
they would all rise to their feet and break into one
of their monotonous, rhythmical dances, with arms
akimbo and heads lolling. And then I thought how
near to the remote atmosphere of the vast country
their life was, and how great a shame it was that
we should break in upon their hallucinated happiness with our alternate frenzies of religion and bloody
war.

And then one day, while we were sitting at lunch
beneath a little mango-tree on the lawn in front
of the *boma*, the grey Vauxhall car drove up and
the general's aide-de-camp came to ask us for some
pills of arsenic and iron. Smuts was going back to
the front. Again we began to feel as if the campaign were getting under weigh. The more I think
of it, the more I realise how the personality of that
one man dominated the whole conduct of the war
in East Africa. And I sometimes wonder what
would have happened if fortune had not carried
him safely through the risks he faced daily, for
though his divisional generals or brigadiers might
well have carried out in detail the broad strategic
movements with which he quartered that wide
country, we should have lacked the enormous

psychical asset which his masterful courage gave us, and I think that we should have endured our deprivations and our sickness with a less happy confidence.

CHAPTER XXI

NEXT day I drove back in an ambulance to Lukigura. The road had not greatly changed, although the little rains had broken down the bridges and embankments above the nullahs. Down in these hollows gangs of pioneers, with the aid of local natives, were toiling with pick and shovel, fortifying the crumbling soil with logs and branches cut from the surrounding bush. Along the side of the way a great number of small depots and bivouacs were scattered. But the only obvious reminder of the passage of time was the body of one of our own trek oxen which had fallen down dead in the forest road past Kangata. On my way in to Handeni I had seen it lying bloated and swollen, now the hide hung loose and shrunken about the flanks, so that gaunt hip bones and ribs showed through. It lay not far from a refilling station of the Supplies and Transport, and though they had not taken the trouble to bury or burn it, I suppose their nearness had kept the hyenas and jackals away.

At Lukigura I found things much as I had left

them. The South African field-guns still lay in the pits which had been digged for them on the day of the fight when their gunners had been so busy taking the imaginary ranges. The Rhodesians were still there, reduced, alas! by now, to less than a hundred and fifty rifles, but cheerful as ever. A battalion of the Cape Coloured Corps had been moved up, and occupied the little ridge on which the German shells had been bursting. At the river itself the Fusiliers were encamped, and at the spot known indifferently as Makindu and M'siha some ten miles beyond the river, General Sheppard lay with the Baluchis, Punjabis and Kashmiris. In this camp he had been rather indolently bombarded by the enemy, now lying safe behind their positions in the N'guru Mountains, and particularly under the shadow of the great hill called Kanga.

At Handeni, on still nights, we had heard the sound of their heavy guns, more than forty-five miles away, and it was said that even the flashes could be seen against the darkness of the hills. At any rate, on the night of my return to Lukigura, Sheppard's column was getting as much as it wanted. Up till this time the enemy had never used their artillery to much advantage. But now that the brigade had been lying at Makindu for

close on three weeks, they had had time not only to
accumulate a head of shell, but, through the advices
of their spies, and direct observation from the over-
hanging hills, to range with accuracy the position
of this perimeter camp, or even more, to map out
the exact space occupied by every unit.   Every day
a few desultory ranging shots had been fired which
did no great harm to anybody, and as they came so
seldom and so haphazard the troops had not been
ordered to dig themselves in.   But on the night of
July the sixth the camp at Makindu was swept by
a methodical and searching fire of high explosive.
From the Cape Corps' ridge we watched their shells
brilliantly bursting.   It was a beautiful sight, even
from that distance, for the air was clear and dry,
and far behind the flashes of bursting shells the
mouths of the guns lit the sky with pale flickers
as of summer lightning.

In the dusk of that evening a little company of
Rhodesian reinforcements marched in.   They had
had a long march of ninety miles or more from railhead, but their bearing was gay and hopeful, as
though the march on Morogoro were to their liking.
They swung gaily into the camp at Lukigura, and
as they turned the corner by the South African
guns, they came face to face with a little company

of grey spectres, men of the regiment, who were dragging slowly to the ambulance on their way back. They staggered along in their overcoats as though the weight of them were almost too much to be borne, and behind them walked the African stretcher-bearers trailing their kits and rifles. The contrast was both strange and terrible.

Next morning we moved off along the river road to join the rest of the brigade at Makindu. It was good, very good, to find myself on trek again, to hear the crack of the Cape-boys' long whips, the measured footsteps of marching men, the rumble of wheels and the jolt and jingle of tossing mule-packs. But we seemed to move more slowly than we used to do, and in a little while I realised the reason for this. I saw that nearly all our mules were sadly wasted, with gaunt hollows in their quarters and strangely hungry faces. Some of them were also puffed beneath their bellies in the way which is pathognomonic of trypanosomiasis; the disease which in humankind we know as sleeping sickness. And our bullocks were little better. Nothing else, indeed, could have been expected as a result of the wait at Lukigura; for driving along the road above the camp in a motor ambulance about the time of sunset I was often bitten by tsetses, and the poor beasts which were grazing in the woodlands must have been infected many times.

Sleeping sickness itself we never saw. I suppose the disease had hardly time to develop in the short months of our trek, but I had often in my mind the potential danger to all that part of Africa of which we traversed the fly belts. Many of our porters came from the Great Lakes, where the disease abounds. We could not be sure that some of them had not the seeds of the malady with them, in which case many of the tsetses in the fly belts might easily become carriers of the disease, and, in the end, all these vast tracks of the continent become uninhabitable to man. Thus, by its great movements of savage peoples, the African War is bound to have spread disease in lands where assuredly there is enough already.

But however alarming the threat to human life may have been, the state of our animals was sufficiently ominous in itself. It suggested that in a very short time we might be wholly without transport ; that, indeed, the whole of our force might be immobilised, for we did not, like the Germans, depend for our mobility on native porterage. All the way to Makindu evidence of the wretched beasts' sufferings was thrust upon us. I even saw a veterinary officer jump from his own horse to examine another in the road and inject it with a dose of arsenic as it stood.

When we came to the Lukigura river itself we saw a noticeboard inscribed in both English and Dutch pointing to the animals' watering-place of the Mounted Brigade. So we knew that Brits was coming. And when Brits has come, we thought, we shall not stay for long under these mountains ; for the cavalry will get in behind them and then the Germans must give us a pitched battle or else throw up the sponge. The reflection was cheering, and yet I couldn't help remembering the tsetse - fly along the Lukigura road, and thinking of Brits's horses.

About the road to Makindu there was nothing very remarkable, except that it might well have been built for the sake of snipers, turning sometimes on itself for a couple of hundred yards at a time, and commanded throughout this length by the wooded hills. All along this way we could see the cleverly prepared positions from which the Germans had planned to fight a long defensive action of which our sudden victory at Lukigura had robbed them. A great deal of art had gone to the fortification of this road : even now, when their green screens were

withered, the machine-gun emplacements were so
concealed that no enemy could have seen them
before he had been swept by their fire. And there
also we saw the pits from which the four-inch shells
had come bursting on the ridge the night after the
battle by the river.

We were thinking little enough of four-inch guns
when we approached Makindu. In their retreat the
Germans had destroyed the bridge by which the
road had crossed the little river named M'siha, which
flows into the Lukigura further south ; and leaving
the wreck of the old bridge where it stood, our
engineers had soon built another a little way down
stream. As we approached the bridgehead—and,
since it was narrow, our column was delayed there—
the enemy opened fire, making the most excellent
practice, on the road leading to the old bridge which
they knew, and which, I suppose, they guessed we
should have repaired. Luckily no damage was
done, but this bombardment was a foretaste of the
particular joys by which Makindu is remembered.

No doubt our higher command realised this, for
the first order that we received on our arrival was
that we should dig ourselves in, a command that
struck us as rather unnecessary, for in those days
we had no great respect for the German artillery.

And that for this reason : that during all the earlier part of the campaign the enemy had been using nothing but armour-piercing shells from the cruiser *Königsberg*, whose armament the naval forces had wholly failed to destroy, and these shells had never done much damage unless they had made a direct hit, the chances of which were reasonably remote. But since the arrival of the cursed blockade runner at Lindi, with its well-chosen cargo of munitions and arms, the naval guns had been supplied with common shell and shrapnel and high explosive, putting a different complexion on the matter altogether.

Under a lazy bombardment of this kind we marched into the Makindu camp, just ahead of the Rhodesians, and settled down in a thin wood with a gentle rise bounded by a steep cliff between us and the river. Rather a pleasant spot it seemed that afternoon, with the air between the trees full of golden light, and to the west of us the soft and lovely outlines of the N'guru hills. And the sky there was of a warm blue, and stainless but for the dissolving clouds, yellow and black, of the bursting shell.

It seemed, as I say, an almost unnecessary precaution to build ourselves dug-outs, for, at the most, we should be there a day or two. Had not Smuts

R

come forward and was not Brits expected by the
Lukigura river? But we stayed in the camp of
Makindu (or M'siha) for a whole month, and I do
not think there was any place in the whole of that
miserable country that became more universally
detested by our troops.

For this there were several reasons, and one of the
greatest, that here we began to reap in the most
alarming degree the harvest of disease which the
Pangani had sown. In the *bandas* which we built
under the trees of the wood our own single ambulance had sometimes as many as three hundred sick
men lying.

At first it was a fairly easy matter to evacuate
them, for the road to Handeni was reasonably good,
and the supply lorries came through regularly. But
when we had lain there a week or two and had not
moved at all, the enemy, emboldened by our inactivity and holding, for that matter, a more secure
position than ourselves with numbers as great,
began a series of small raids on our communications
which made their maintenance perilous, and more
than once put us in doubt of our supplies, and some
anxiety as to our own standing. For Makindu,
being thrust in between the foot of the mountains
which the enemy held and the Lukigura which in

its southern bend he also commanded, and faced by the Kanga position astride of the road which he had blocked and mined and measured with his heavy guns, was a possession of some peril, and the more so when we heard of raids in the neighbourhood of Kangata : motor lorries blown to atoms, an ambulance convoy mined, and even stories of a threat to our station at Handeni. The latter, indeed, was the gravest of all, for if Handeni were threatened where in the world were we ?

It did not increase our sense of confidence when the whole of Hannyngton's Brigade was whisked back from the Lukigura, to which it had advanced, to deal with the isolated forces of the enemy who had abandoned the lower Tanga line, and even dared to attack our railhead at Korogwe. In this business the supply lorries were so busy that we had no convoys for several days, while Handeni itself had a grievous fright and laboured so thoroughly at earthwork fortifications that when I saw it next I hardly knew it.

In the end it amounted to this : that the enemy lay on three sides of us ; that we were sick and tired ; and that we could not move. If we had moved, if we had suddenly found ourselves caught up in another of those fine, sweeping movements by which

R 2

we had already conquered Kilimanjaro and swept down the Pangani to clear the Tanga line, I believe our ills and our preoccupations would both have been relieved. At any rate, there was something a little inspiring in the thought that the greatest of the enemy forces was in front of us, that things were really blowing up for a big battle.

We were fed on rumours, often vilely untrue. But at the same time there came to us news of exploits on the part of our own intelligence department which were brilliant enough to brighten a very dull time, and one in particular which equalled the finest achievements of Pretorius in its daring. This was the journey of the three agents, Weinholt, Lewis, and Browne to the Central Railway. These men left the camp at Lukigura on June the 28th, and returned to Makindu on the 21st of July. At first they steered due west, and very quickly got in touch with the enemy who were driving in cattle from all the villages on our right flank south of Handeni. These they evaded with difficulty, only to find themselves in the path of another company encamped about a waterhole on the western base of the N'guru Mountains, which now lay between them and our forces. Here, again, they miraculously escaped, making a combined report on the

nature of the country, and trekking almost due
south over a hilly and dry land. In this neighbourhood they fell in with bands of raiding Masai who
were repaying themselves for the Germans' depre-
dations of their cattle by attacks on isolated home-
steads. In one place they found a great fire and
the charred remains of men with deep spear wounds.
From there they pushed south again, and in the
deep bush country above the Wami river they
stumbled on an enemy convoy of a hundred porters
carrying ammunition, clothing, wines, and tobacco
to the front. This convoy they raided single-
handed, terrifying the porters and compelling them
to make a bonfire of all those goods that they could
not carry away. Three of the askaris who were
guarding the convoy they made prisoners, and
carried along with them on their way further south.

At last they reached a spot from which they could
see the Central Railway, the object of our invasion,
and when they had stayed there a little while and
contented themselves with all the observations
which they could take, they turned their faces northward once more. But now they were the best part
of a hundred miles from our forces, and between them
and us lay a great gathering of all the enemy's
strength. It was part of their work, however, to

learn as much as possible of the German communications, and while they were engaged in this most
hazardous work, by the Wami river, their party
was rushed by a considerable body of the enemy,
and in the running fight Weinholt was lost.

From this point their journey became most
perilous, for now the Germans knew exactly with
what they had to deal. Travelling by night, and
with the greatest caution, they continued their
way northward, cutting all enemy telegraph wires
as they came upon them. On the 21st of July,
five days after the surprise at the Wami, in which
they had lost all their food and kit, Browne and
Lewis struggled, half dead with fatigue and starvation, into our camp at Makindu. They had worked
their way up the banks of the Lukigura, and had
been guided to our camp by the enemy's shell fire.
And with them into the camp at Makindu they
brought their three prisoners. Of Weinholt nothing
more was heard for many weeks.

Perhaps it was because of this exploit that the
enemy artillery paid so much attention to the headquarters of the intelligence department, which stood
on the bank of the river behind the Rhodesians'
lines. After the first night of our arrival they soon
showed us that they could place their shells wherever

they liked in our camp, and the big *bandas* which we built for our patients, and which their spies must surely have described to them as a hospital, came in for more than their share. It had been the same with Van Deventer's force when they lay at Kondoa Irangi. With the utmost regularity, every other day, and invariably also on Sundays, they bombarded the Makindu camp, taking a steady toll of casualties in beasts and men in spite of our dugouts. By this time they had learned the trick of firing their naval guns at an extreme range of more than eleven thousand yards, by digging a great pit for the gun's mounting and tilting it so that they obtained something very nearly resembling the high-angle fire of a howitzer, against which our cover was of little value. And so expert did they become in their calculation of our range, that they managed to burst their high explosives very low down below the level of the tree tops, and in this way did us a great deal of damage.

The favourite time for these bombardments was eleven o'clock at night, at a time when we were settling off to sleep. For an hour or more they would give us a heavy, searching fire, and then case off to the rate of one shell every half-hour, and later one every hour, which was just enough to keep us awake, or to bring us casualties for dressing all night long. No doubt the use of their big guns put heart into their askaris. At Lukigura, when they bombarded us at night, our askari prisoners, and indeed the Germans as well, were terrified at the explosions of their own shells upon the ridge. They had been assured by their leaders that with every shot we lost many lives, and no doubt this assurance was used as a sort of moral antidote to the fear inspired by our 'bird's' visitations. Moreover, even though the damage their fire did us at Makindu was not great materially, I think it was of moral value to the enemy; not because we were afraid of it, but because we were unable to reply to it. We had no artillery at the front which could get anywhere near the stations of the naval guns. Our only possible reply—and though its effect was uncertain it certainly helped to raise our spirits—was bombardment from the air. One day, after a particularly heavy and effective fire at night, in one of those golden, cloudless evenings of Makindu, five of our planes came drifting down from the north, very beautiful in their gleaming white, and in a few minutes forty bombs were dropped. We watched them, clustered on the hill which had been called Kashmiri Kopje, and their explosions were as balm to our spirits; for the

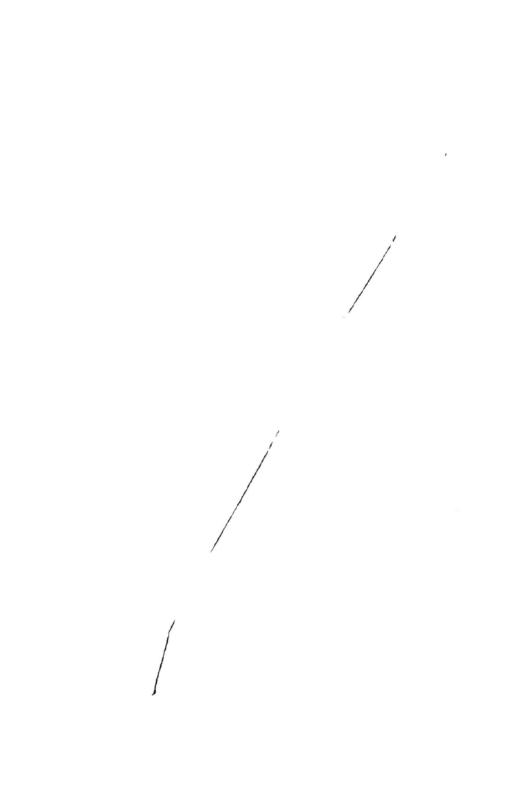

mountains began to play with their echoing sound, so that each bomb made a detonation which sounded like the bouncing of a gigantic metal football. Boo-oo-oom ... bom ·. . bom ... bom . . . bom. . . . But that night they gave us a reiterated assurance that the big guns were undamaged.

The Rhodesians, the Punjabis, and the unfortunate 17th Cavalry suffered most ; for they all encamped in an open space, just south of the river, which must have been clearly visible from the mountains. Gradually the whole of this area became too hot for habitation, and the various units moved their camping-grounds into the grooved valleys in the side of Kashmiri Kopje where the battery mules were already sheltered. And at last we moved with them. Life in the old low camp at Makindu was becoming more and more unpleasant. The enemy observers were quick to catch sight of any movement on the road ; and the motor ambulance convoy invariably evacuated our sick and wounded under fire. The German gunners had a pretty trick of skimming the tops of our *bandas* and bursting on the road beyond, where the ambulances were drawn up.

It was rather trying for a man who had been already wounded in the field to be wounded again in hospital ; and so we chose a site in a deep valley

upon the far side of the kopje where the hillside
sloped at an angle of 'one in four,' and the peak
rose several hundred feet between us and the enemy.
Here, the gunners told us, we should be almost certainly safe. We terraced all the hillside, with the
aid of the pioneers, and moved there close on two
hundred sick. And the first day that we entered
into possession the enemy dropped a four-inch shell
right into our new hospital.

There was a good deal of humour in the situation,
but it meant a renewal of our digging. In two days
the pioneers had made us dug-out accommodation
with head cover to the thickness of three feet of
earth and two layers of hardwood trunks, for all our
patients.

And then the news came that Van Deventer had
moved. This was all that we had been waiting for.
Suddenly he had advanced from Kondoa Irangi,
clearing the enemy positions with the bayonet, and
even now three columns were bearing down upon the
Central Railway to west of us. The whole atmosphere of the camp at Makindu abruptly changed.
The naval guns which had been lying at M'buyuni
were now at railhead and the Germans would soon
be outranged. But now we cared for none of these
things. Our weary days of waiting were over.

In two days the pioneers had made us dug-out accommodation for all our patients (*p.* 256)

CHAPTER XXII

BUT it was not for me to enjoy this fruition. For four days I listened to the Germans' bombardment from my bed in one of the dug-outs which I had watched the pioneers make. It was a dreary time, and five weeks of fever do not make one see things at their best. I lay there, beneath the surface of the earth, watching, through a sort of window, the platforms below me, on which two hundred other sick were placed, and below them a great tangle of brushwood, the dry bed of a stream, and tall trees hung with lianas between. I think that my principal diversion, apart from the curiosity which arose from the fact that now I could not see where the enemy's shells were falling, was a family of long-tailed monkeys, who had made their home in the trees of that gully ; and two in particular, paragons of marital devotion, whom I could watch in the first grey of the morning, sitting side by side upon a horizontal branch with arms interlocked, very still, like lovers on a bench in the park.

They were all weary days ; always the same

gunfire in the dead of night; the same bomb-
dropping birds in the golden afternoon; the same
processions of sick Indians moving about very slowly
over the hillside, wrapped in their grey blankets.
And these were rather an irritating sight, for when
an Indian is ill, no matter how little there may be the
matter with him, he droops like a cut flower. In a
little while I had learned exactly what these languish-
ing airs were worth, and the sight of them was not
soothing to a sick man's nerves.

On the fifth day the motor ambulance convoy was
expected, but did not turn up. On the sixth day,
just as we were awaiting it, at midday, the Germans,
for no reason of which we were aware, started a particularly vicious bombardment of the M'siha river:
our most precious water. When the firing began
the convoy had been back at Lukigura, and there
they stayed until the German gunners knocked off
for lunch, arriving at Makindu about two o'clock.
We were hurried into the ambulances at the bottom
of the hill, and crossed the M'siha bridge exactly
as the enemy reopened fire with a shell upon the
old bridge road. All the way to Lukigura I heard
the sound of the bombardment. At that distance it
seemed almost more impressive than it had been
within range, and I must admit that it was a great

relief to feel safe outside a dug-out. But I would
have given anything in the world, as the convoy
rolled away, to have been well and strong, and
ready to move out on the trek for which we had
halted so long.

Even the short drive to Lukigura was a painful
matter for a sick man, for the road was by this time
atrocious, and the Ford ambulance in which I
travelled was almost down on its axles for want of
springs. At Lukigura—remembering the fate of
the last convoy which had travelled by night and
had lost a car blown to atoms by a road mine—we
lay that night. For some reason or other it was
appallingly cold.

All through the early part of the night we heard
the German guns firing on Makindu, and wondered how our fellows were faring; and in the
small hours of the morning we heard other gunfire,
heavier and very distant, which we knew must be a
naval bombardment somewhere on the coast. Our
thoughts turned to Dar-es-Salaam. Perhaps a force
was landing there even now, under cover of the
naval guns. That, indeed, should be the beginning
of the end; but I smiled to remember what Smuts
was reported to have said when, at an earlier date,
this landing had been pressed upon him by one of his

generals : ' I don't want any more of this amphibious
nonsense.' And certainly he had done well enough
so far without it ; but the thought of another force
working up from the south was sufficiently inspiring.
Ah, why must I be out of it ?

Next morning we jolted on to Handeni. The old
road, which now I knew so well, was patrolled in all
its length by little pickets of the Cape Corps, and
we heard that the reason for this was that Smuts
was coming forward again and that road mines were
feared. I think that this was the first time that
I ever heard of the general submitting to any cares
for his personal safety. In other ways the road was
much the same except for its surface, which was
worse. And for the fourth time, hard by Kangata,
I saw the body of my trek ox, now reduced to a
heap of hide and bone.

It was not an enlivening journey, for all the land
through which we passed was now so deeply scarred
with the wreck and ruin of war, with patches of
bush blackened by fire, with the vast litter of
deserted camps, with great trees felled by the
wayside and left alone with fires still smouldering
in their trunks and green leaves withered, with the
bodies of dead beasts scattered along the roadside,
and the stench of others which we could not see.

Even more terrible than the dead were the living.
Twice in the course of our journey to Handeni, and
once, three days later on the road beyond, we fell
in with the most piteous convoys of horses and mules
condemned for trypanosomiasis. They were all
dreadfully thin and weak; their coats showed the
peculiar lack of condition which you see in a sick
animal, and many already bore that fatal swelling
in the abdominal wall with which I was only too
well acquainted. All of these creatures wore on
their necks a red veterinary ticket. I think they
were more pathetic because one felt that they didn't
know what was happening to them; that the
Dutchmen in charge of them were driving them back
to Korogwe to die just because it would be easier
there to get rid of their poor, wasted bodies. I
watched them struggling weakly into the bush,
tugging at the grass here and there in a futile desire
to live. And once I saw two that had fallen down,
not half-way through their pilgrimage, and would
not move for the drivers' whips. A miserable, miserable business. . . .

Three days I spent at Handeni; then travelling
on again to railhead (Korogwe) over a more abominable surface than ever, we reached the conquered
Tanga line. It was good to remember that it was

we who had conquered it. We lay in an iron truck
of the kind which is cryptically labelled ' N.B.X.' on
heaps of sisal flax, from the factories at Korogwe,
piled above the rotten droppings of mules. The
bed was soft enough, but full of fleas. And we
lived for the most part on tea made with water
which we begged from the engine-driver. For a
day and a night we struggled up the Tanga line,
and night and day, other and more important trains
went clanking past us, carrying not stores nor ammunition, nor men, but only transport beasts, oxen and
mules, wedged tightly in the same sort of trucks as
ourselves—healthy animals being swiftly carried
into a land where death awaited them, or worse
than death, the lingering weakness of the wretched
beasts whom we had seen walking back to die at
Korogwe. And yet I wished I could go with them.
In a week those same creatures might well be pushing through the foothills of the N'guru, or trekking
down the Lukigura towards the greater Wami, on
' the old trail, the out trail, the trail that is always
new . . .' and with them would go old comrades
of mine. Not so very old . . . but the common
sufferings of war weld friendships between man and
man that are most precious things, and bonds that
death too often severs suddenly. I knew that

many, nay, most of these friends, I should never see
again.

. . . . . .

We were winding slowly up a little gradient close
under the escarpment of the Pare Mountains, and
the station which we had just left behind was Buiko.
In a few minutes we should be in sight of that bottle
neck from which the Rhodesians had forced the
Germans at our first encounter. I remembered it
all with a little thrill, for it was here, too, that I
had first been under fire. And then I remembered
the golden days down the Pangani, those rich, star-
powdered nights, the long talks over a dying fire,
the smell of wood smoke. And ' Not one of us,' I
thought, ' will ever visit these strange wildernesses
again. Many of us for the reason that we shall
not be alive. But even if we are alive, we shall
not see the upper reaches of the Pangani, for no
man in his senses would visit them twice. This
country without a soul. . . .' And then I thought
of the strangeness with which our immense consciousness, of ten thousand men, had been flashed
across the vast and sombre vacuity of these tracts
of rolling bush and plain over which the shadow of a
man's spirit had never moved before ; and of how
that consciousness had traversed it, as a dream

wanders through a man's mind in sleep. But, though we do not always know it, the submerged memory of the dream lingers. And, in the same way, it seemed to me that though the forest tangles of the Pangani close above the tracks we made, and the blown sand fill our trenches and drift above the graves of those whom we left sleeping there, that ancient, brooding country can never be the same again, nor wholly desert, now that so many men have lived intensely for a little while in its recesses. Shall we not revisit the Pangani, I and many others, the country to which we have given a soul?

KABETE, 1916.

A FAREWELL TO AFRICA

Now once again, upon the pole-star's bearing
We plough these furrowed fields where no blade springeth;
Again the busy trade in the halyards singeth
Sun-whitened spindrift from the blown wave shearing;
The uncomplaining sea suffers our faring;
In a brazen glitter our little wake is lost,
And the starry south rolls over until no ghost
Remaineth of us and all our pitiful daring;
For the sea beareth no trace of man's endeavour,
His might enarmoured, his prosperous argosies,
Soundless within her unsounded caves for ever
She broodeth, knowing neither war nor peace,
And our grey cruisers holds in mind no more
Than the cedarn fleets that Sheba's treasure bore.

Off MOMBASA,
  February 1917.

GLASGOW: W. COLLINS SONS AND CO. LTD.

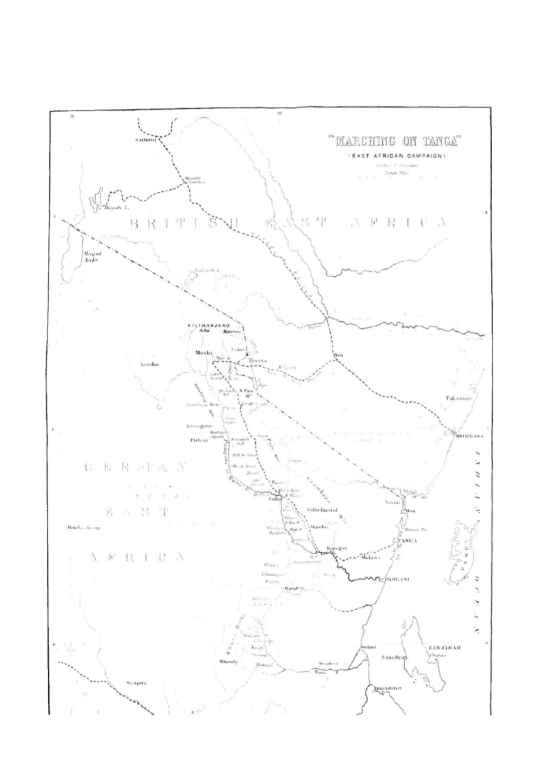

"MARCHING ON TANGA"
(EAST AFRICAN CAMPAIGN)